INTO THE GREEN

A RECONNAISSANCE BY FIRE

CHEROKEE PAUL McDONALD

A PLUME BOOK

PLUME
Published by the Penguin Group
Penguin Putnam Inc., 375 Hudson Street, New York, New York 10014, U.S.A.
Penguin Books Ltd, 27 Wrights Lane, London W8 5TZ, England
Penguin Books Australia Ltd, Ringwood, Victoria, Australia
Penguin Books Canada Ltd, 10 Alcorn Avenue, Toronto, Ontario, Canada M4V 3B2
Penguin Books (N. Z.) Ltd, 182–190 Wairau Road, Auckland 10, New Zealand

Penguin Books Ltd, Registered Offices:
Harmondsworth, Middlesex, England

First published by Plume,
a member of Penguin Putnam Inc.

First Printing, July 2001
10 9 8 7 6 5 4 3 2 1

Ⓡ REGISTERED TRADEMARK — MARCA REGISTRADA

LIBRARY OF CONGRESS CATALOGING-IN-PUBLICATION DATA:

McDonald, Cherokee Paul.
   Into the green : a reconnaissance by fire / Cherokee Paul McDonald.
      p.   cm.
   ISBN 0-452-28252-7
      1. Vietnamese Conflict, 1961–1975—Personal narratives, American.
      2. Vietnamese Conflict, 1961–1975—Reconnaissance operations, American.
      3. McDonald, Cherokee Paul.   I. Title.
   DS559.5.M399   2001
   959.704'3'092—dc21   00-048368

Printed in the United States of America
Set in Janson Text

BOOKS ARE AVAILABLE AT QUANTITY DISCOUNTS WHEN USED TO PROMOTE PRODUCTS OR
SERVICES. FOR INFORMATION PLEASE WRITE TO PREMIUM MARKETING DIVISION, PENGUIN
PUTNAM INC., 375 HUDSON STREET, NEW YORK, NEW YORK 10014.

Praise  onald's

"Cherokee takes no prisoners in this finely imagined . . . honest book . . . and . . . and . . . some of it by making . . . . It's . . . God for us that Ch . . . . back . . . with all his faculties and . . . . out in the country . . . . re, it's a book yo . . . ."

—John Dufresne, author of *Louisiana Power and Light*

"A riveting journey back to a time and place that marked a generation and changed the world forevermore. Former First Lt. Cherokee Paul McDonald is a gifted and perceptive writer . . . William Wordsworth maintained that the very best writing arises from intense emotion recollected in tranquility—he must have seen Cherokee coming."

—Les Standiford, author of *Black Mountain*
and *Deal with the Dead*

And for McDonald's previous work
Blue Truth

"His unforgettable memoir rings with gripping authenticity."
—*Booklist*

Summer's Reason

"Fans of the late John McDonald will experience a nostalgic flashback. McDonald's work grows ever more sure-handed."
—*The Cleveland Plain Dealer*

CHEROKEE PAUL MCDONALD is the author of three novels and an acclaimed memoir, *Blue Truth*. His articles have appeared in the *Fort Lauderdale Sun-Sentinel*, among other publications. He lives in Florida.

For
Corporal Walter Guy "Butchy" Burkhart,
"C" Company, 75th Infantry (Ranger),
Killed in Action, November 1969,
Binh Thuy Province, Vietnam;
&
Lieutenant David E. Palanzi,
"C" Company, 1/8th Infantry,
Fourth Infantry Division,
Pleiku, Vietnam:
Still Charging On.

War is best in memory.

INTRODUCTION

THE stories in this book happened when I was a bright and shiny young soldier. I was an idealist, an awkward romantic, a believer . . . fresh-faced, healthy, and smart enough to know there was a lot about life I did not understand and had not yet experienced. I was hungry for those experiences, willing to venture to a hard place where war existed. Thirty years have passed, and I am no longer bright and shiny. I am the sum total of my days and nights, and they can be seen in my eyes. My face is a contour map of the war and of the coming home. It reflects the topography of a heart rich in the hard experiences once longed for.

I subtitled this book *A Reconnaissance by Fire*. A recon is an exploratory military survey of enemy territory. To recon by fire is to sit in defilade, back in the cool shadows of jungle or time, and fire into enemy territory or layers of emotion. You know you have to cross open ground to get to where they are. You will be exposed; their fire will seek you out, wound you, kill you. You don't simply stroll out there into the sun, into the past. You fire a few rounds into a dark wedge of tangled vine, put a burst into the crease in the jungle where a small streambed lies, lob a couple of grenades into the trees that stand like protesters along the edge of an apparently benign rice paddy. Then you wait for reaction from the hidden enemy. Your fire might cause them to move; perhaps they will return fire, or maybe one of your rounds will set off a secondary explosion in their ammunition. Either way, you'll know. You'll be able to gauge their strength, their firepower, their ability to hurt you. You want to go into the green, but first you must recon.

So it was for me when I decided to venture back. My memories were there, waiting in the recesses of my mind, and I prepared to go there, to write them. Like the memories of many combat veterans, my memories of war remained tightly wrapped in an asbestos shroud and tucked safely away in the dark. The years went by; then, with an unarguable certainty, I realized it was time to write about the Vietnam I had experienced. As soon as I took one or two cautious steps on a patrol through the past I realized the folly of blithely walking back into the green. The sudden flash of a tracer-fire memory sent me twisting down, and as I fell, shrapnel images left blood trails across my heart. I dragged myself back to the relative safety of the shadows, regrouped, and decided on another approach. A recon by fire.

I began to explore the memories, and as I did I decided to write them as they came, to tell the stories in the voice of memory. Memory does not return in textbook or journal fashion; it is often not supported by careful research regarding names, dates, places . . . specific units, battles, enemy designations, commanders, strategies, and objectives. There might be the grinning face of a guy who turned to say something to you just before he disappeared in an explosion, or the still and silent tableau of bodies in the wire. It might come as a smell, some evil odor that triggers the memory of a low crawl across a forever rice paddy, or the fish heads and rice vomited up by a dying child. A sound can trigger it. The click of a child's toy and the soft, sibilant snick of a well-oiled rifle bolt become one, and with it the jolting memory of fear and anticipation.

I knew I could not write a documented, researched, by-the-numbers military memoir. When I was in Vietnam I paid little attention to those details. I did not keep a journal, I simply lived the experiences. As a writer going back, I found the *moments* most important . . . taste, texture, color, smell, emotion. It might be impossible to capture war with words, the essence, the reality, the purity of it. Many writers come as close as they can by using known identifiers. They validate their discourse by carefully setting time and place, dates and locations of battles, units, names of those who fought there. They do their best to capture war by means of a straight-forward account of who was there and what they did. Many events in war, horrific, brutal, heroic, frightening, uplifting, or devastating, can be captured by a clean recounting of the action. Certainly this is true of acts of courage or self-sacrifice. Neither rich prose nor descriptive embroidery is needed to describe a man rising above his fears, placing himself in mortal danger to accomplish a goal, and perhaps giving his life as he triumphs. I chose to try to help the reader taste the essence of war in a less documentary or journalistic style.

This leaves me, and my memories, open to critical speculation. Sure, a reader might think, these are interesting stories about the war in Vietnam, but are they real? Fiction is nice, and a writer can cover a lot of fertile ground through fiction, but war is *not* fiction, and I want to read about war. Can the writer and his work be validated?

I joined the Army in June 1966, one year out of high school. My draft status was 1A, but that didn't matter; there was a war in Vietnam, and I wanted to go there. I went through Basic Training at Fort Benning, Georgia. The Infantry suited me and I desired nothing special; I simply wanted to soldier. I tested well, however, and was offered a chance at Officer Candidate School. I took it, and went to OCS at the Artillery School in Fort Sill, Oklahoma. I was commissioned as a Second Lieutenant in 1967, and learned the basics of my craft and rank with the First Armored Division, Fort Hood, Texas. I finally got my orders to Vietnam in January 1968, right after the Tet Offensive, and was assigned to the First Field Forces, II Corps, Central Highlands. My parent unit was Battery A, Third Battalion, Sixth Artillery, First Field Forces. I say "parent unit" because I was a Forward Observer ("FO," or "FAO"). I was assigned a Recon Sergeant and an RTO (Radio/Telephone Operator), and spent my eleven months in Vietnam hitchhiking all around the Highlands on temporary duty with different units who needed an FO team for specific operations or situations. I worked with units of the 173rd Airborne, the Fourth Infantry Division, the Third ARVN (Army of the Republic of Vietnam) Armored, and various Special Forces A-Teams and their Montagnard soldiers around Plei Me, Plei Mrong, and Duc Co. I worked along Highway 19 from An Khe through the Mang Yang Pass to Pleiku, and mostly west of Highway 14 between Pleiku, Kontum, and Dak To. I was in the mountains along the Cambodian border, and in the Ia Drang Valley.

Because I did not have an actual base camp, I spent almost all of my time in the field. Usually my team was sent to where there was a *need* for us, so my combat experiences were rich. I worked with the Green Berets, but was not flash-qualified (a graduate of their Special Warfare School). I was not a Navy

SEAL, Marine Sniper, or an LRRP (Long Range Recon Patrol), and I did not do spooky things with Air America. I was a soldier, a glorified grunt with artillery connections. I saw perhaps more action than some, less than others. Mobility and variety were the true gifts of my assignments, and I embraced them. I received a couple of commendations. After eleven months in-country I was medevaced from the 51st Medevac Unit in Pleiku to Camp Zama Hospital, Japan, then sent home in early 1969.

I was not alone during my tour. I worked with other guys who were basically young men from the World trying to survive a year in Vietnam. My primary partners in war were men I call Recon and RTO. They were not the same two guys throughout my time in-country. Rather than name them to fit the varied memories, I simply used their descriptive titles from one story to the next. Each soldier takes on the personality of his rank and job. To me, a man named Recon is immediately a Recon Sergeant: solid, dependable, a veteran of combat and military bullshit, a man of strength and patience. An RTO is a different type, garrulous, inquisitive, slightly rebellious and irreverent, tied for better or worse to his radio and his LT (lieutenant). I have spent many nights in the triple canopy with both of these men. They walk my memories with me, and I gave the faces in memory names representative of their breed. The only real names I've used are those of Corporal Walter Guy "Butchy" Burkhart, an LRRP with the 75th Rangers, and Lieutenant David Palanzi, an FO with the Fourth Infantry Division . . . and those names are as real as Butchy's grave, and as the shrapnel still embedded in David's flesh.

Everything in this book is real, and happened during the war in Vietnam. It either happened to me, or I was there and saw it, or I was a small part of it, or I was in direct communication with people who *did* it. The stories come from my memories, not my imagination. In some stories I use dialogue. Do I remember each conversation word for word? No. I remember the circumstances of the exchange, the faces, the heart and focus of the discussion, and I attempted to write them as accurately as possible. The clearest indicia of truth in these stories will be the shared experiences. Other veterans of the war will recognize situations comparable to what they saw, heard, or did. I chose to handle my memories as a writer, an older man examining the actions, experiences, and emotions of a younger man. Perhaps I was more warrior-poet than journalist, and if in poetry many truths can be found within carefully chosen words, so be it.

Enough.

Come with me now.

Watch your spacing and noise discipline.

Listen.

Fort Lauderdale, Florida
May 2000

INTO THE GREEN

Prologue

I WAITED impatiently for the orders that would send me to war in Vietnam. Vietnam waited too, a mystical and savage land where small ferocious people with tilted eyes and yellow skin, dressed in black pajamas for their nightmare, made war with themselves and waited for me to join in. Much of the war was fought in the jungle, a deep, dark, impenetrable mystery . . . a place of brutal life, violent death, and sinister potential. It was a place made exotic by its name, Vietnam. It was a place I had to go; it called to me, sang to me, whispered to me.

When the orders finally came I held them in trembling hands and swept them carefully with my hungry eyes. They had a certain weight and energy, I realized, powerful enough to transport my body and soul from one reality to another. I held them with my fingertips, much like an old book taken from a library shelf and opened to the first page. I stared at the words, and saw the old book was written in a language I did not yet understand.

Bright and Shiny

DID a timeless thing, like in the movies, on my way to war.

It was the summer of 1966, and I had joined the Army. We traveled from the induction center in Coral Gables, where we took our physicals and a battery of written exams ("You will take the one-each number two leaded pencil in your hand. If you write with your left hand you will place the number two leaded pencil in your left hand. If you write with your *right* hand you will . . ."), to Fort Benning, Georgia, by train. We still had our hair, our civilian personalities. Some of us were cocky, loud, expounding on what it would be like in the Army and how well we would do. Some of us were quiet, scared, unsure. Most of us had butterflies, a sense of excitement, a sense of *going* somewhere, *doing* something.

The train ride was pleasant. Box lunches and black porters who were politely patient and said "Yassirr" with a touch of sadness. We were southern boys, but most of us felt slightly awkward having men old enough to be our fathers waiting on us. One of us had a harmonica, one of us had a million jokes, one of us delighted in playing tricks on everybody. All of us had great stories of the successes we had already had with "women." Stories of girls past and Vietnam future were equal in frequency and intensity, the first a mixture of fact and wishful bravado, the second a mixture of hope and dread.

More than once I stared at my reflection in the glass window and remembered the last real conversation I had with my father. I had marched boldly into our small house, faced him, and told him what I had done.

"You joined the Army? For what? Joined the Army for what?" he asked.

"The war," I responded. "The war in Vietnam."

"Ah, ya dumb son of a bitch."

"I joined up, Dad, and I'm goin' . . ."

"How many times have I told you about wars? Wars are a bunch of *bullshit* . . . bullshit money-making ploys that take the tough and smart young guys like you and waste 'em. You know I told pansy FDR to jam it up his ass, don't you? And that was for the *big* one, like your uncle calls it, the big Whiskey Whiskey Two, goddammit. I wouldn't *go* to their war . . . crap . . . all those big-mouthed rich politicians. Oh yeah, I went down to the induction center with a bunch of guys, stood bare-assed in front of five of 'em, colonels and majors . . . asking me questions because I got the languages, and they knew they could use me. I told 'em to stick it up their ass. Right to their faces. Didn't want any part of it because it was all bullshit. I refused, and I went home—"

"Mom told us you went off on the train with all the other guys, flags flying, girls waving, crowds cheering you on. Said you came walking back down those same tracks all alone at four in the morning, because you failed the physical. Dad, you were a four-F."

"Goddamned right I was four-F, because I *wanted* to be. Your mom was there, huh, was there on those railroad tracks at four in the morning?"

"Dad, college isn't for me, you know it. I'm spinning my wheels—"

"Then hit the road. *Go* somewhere, *do* something. Jump your ass onto a tramp steamer and do sailor's work out to Singapore or Australia or someplace like that. Ride the rails out west like I did, to Jackson Hole . . . work a forestry crew, drive a truck, get into a few bar fights, pull the pants off a few leggy women along the way. *Live*, dammit, don't march off to some rich man's war like a dummy."

"Dad, it's war, a war . . . *my* . . . I mean, war in my lifetime, and I want to be part of it, I want to *see* it, experience it . . . see if I can . . . see if I can . . ."

"If you can *what*? If you can be a man? You gotta find out if you're a man by going to a goddamned war? What bullshit."

Card games during the day, lots of bullshit stories, lots of roughhousing. Had our small berth during the night, with the old black men, severe and distinguished, wishing us each a "G'night, suh" as they passed the berth. Had the clackety-clack, clackety-clack, the mournful whistle, and the slowly rolling countryside just like you're supposed to on that kind of train trip. Hey, America . . . we're your *boys*, goin' to be *soldiers*, goin' to *war* . . . goin' off to be brushed by the purple wind. Sometimes somebody in a pickup truck would honk and wave as we rumbled past, but mostly the cars sat in line at the crossings in steamed and impatient silence, tolerating our passage so we would be gone from their world and they could go back to life at *that point*. We rumbled right on past you, America.

"C'mon, Dad . . . since we were kids we been hearin' about Uncle Steve and D Day and big John Wayne, hittin' the beach and takin' that hill. About Patton and the Russians and the Berlin Wall and Communism . . . how Communism is all about tearin' us down, tearin' down what we stand for . . . tearin' down America."

"Tearing down America? What in the hell do you even know about America? Why don't you get on that goddamned motorcycle of yours and ride out there and *find* America? You think the Russians with their Communism can tear this country down? They can't find their ass with both hands. They can't even make a *car*, for chrissakes."

"Dad. I joined. It's the war . . . the war against Communism . . ."

"Goddammit, when the raggedy-ass Chinese come ashore and charge across the highway machine-gunning people in *this* town, then you pick up a rifle and go out and fight Communism. You dumb son of a bitch. You're gonna break your mother's heart."

"Dad. There's a war in Vietnam. I gotta go to it."

"Go over to that shelf, freedom fighter, get the atlas, open it up and point with one of your dumbass fingers. Show me on the map where Vietnam *is*. You can't, can you? You don't know a thing about it, about the people, their culture, their history, their religion, what they're all about. . . ."

"I know the good people there are tryin' to be free, and the ones from the north are tryin' to make 'em all into Commies."

"Did you know the fight-with-your-feet-and-fuck-with-your-face *French* went marching in there after the war with our blessing like it was going to be business as usual and the Vietnamese people kicked their sorry asses right out of there? Did you know?"

"We're not the French, we're the American Army. And we're not tryin' to colonize the place, we're tryin' to *free* it."

"You gonna free them from *themselves*? Good boys are gonna go there, our good boys, and they're gonna *die*, and for what? For what? Your mother always worried you were gonna be a priest, walk around sprinkling holy water, hearing confessions, acting like you actually *knew* Jesus. But no, not you—you decide to go off to war. Christ, I don't know which is worse."

"I want to go see, Dad . . ."

"You're gonna break your mother's heart."

"Dad. I go down to the processing center next week, Tuesday, early . . ."

"You signed the papers, everything formal and all that?"

"I'm *in*, Dad. I signed up, and I'm goin'."

"All right. I'll drive you down."

Our train made a stop outside Waycross, Georgia. We were allowed to get off and wander around the trackside for a few minutes, test the air, change our water, stretch our legs. A train going the other way stopped across from ours, and I found myself looking through a window at that pretty young woman in the summer dress, the one with fresh honey-colored hair brushed back from her flawless face, pouty mouth with red lips, big brown eyes, and long lashes. You've seen her. She works at the corner drugstore, isn't always a cheerleader, marries a hardworking man from the same town, and has healthy, pretty babies. She's the female *us* . . . the one who becomes Mom, the one who wants a new fridge but makes do with the one she has, the one who drives the old sedan so her husband can have the new pickup truck. The one you see at church, at parent-teacher nights. The one who grows into a strong and mature woman, straight, proud, and faithful. The one who holds this whole damned thing together.

She was pretty, older than I, and we had made eye contact. I was backed by a crowd of guys who saw her, too, who saw her see *me*, and who could not let it go. They began punching each other and hooting even *before* she pointed one delicate finger toward the end of her car and got up from her seat.

I met her on the landing between the two cars, climbed up strongly in my jeans and button-down shirt, my confidence generated by the moment and propelling me into a conversation with her. She smiled a lot. I guess I grinned. I watched her eyes. She took my hand and my mouth went dry. The testosterone-fueled and entertainment-starved peanut gallery behind me on my train went wild. They shouted advice and approval, urging me on. Our words bumped into each other. She was on her way somewhere . . . family, school, a job. I was on my way to war.

"Too bad I have to keep going today." She sighed as she took my other hand. She stood so close her high breasts brushed against my shirt. "And too bad you have to keep going the other way." Maybe she was being bold in the safety of the impossibility of the moment; I don't know. I *do* know she added, "Too bad we can't just step off these trains and spend the night together here in, um . . . Waycross . . ."

"Uh, yeah . . . I mean, *yes*," I croaked as the blood rushed to my face and other places. "Too bad."

Then came the movie part.

"Aawhllaah*bow*aard!" Her train lurched and began to move east slowly, me still on the landing with her. My train bumped and began to move west, my peanut gallery whistling and yelling behind me. She leaned forward and kissed me on the lips quickly, gone before I knew it had happened. I stepped down and back, onto the last step, as her train picked up speed. Then she put her warm soft hands on the side of my upturned face, leaned to me, and kissed me long and hot.

There was yelling, I know that, and movement, and train noise and whistles and a sense of powerful machinery groaning off inexorably toward some unknown destination. There was her face, too, her eyes, those lips, the taste of her, the warmth of her, the promise of her. My head was spinning when she finally let me go. The smile she wore as I jumped off the step onto the gravel bed was that all-powerful, all-knowing, all-everything female smile that has made men act the way men act since . . . well, since the beginning. She stood in the landing smiling and waving, and I caught my balance, turned, and ran after my own train, which was pulling out smartly toward the war I was fixin' to miss while I dallied with the lass.

Not to worry. Just like in the movie, my gang of cutthroats was there for me, backed by a grinning black conductor. With whistles, yells, and reaching hands they grabbed me as I ran alongside and pulled me back into the green, pounding my arms and back, laughing in my face, happy to be witness to such a . . . good thing . . . all of them wishing they were me.

A few minutes later, when we were settled in our seats, the girl and her train long gone, the after-action critique began.

"Man, did you see the way she looked at you?"

"Did you see her smile?"

"Did you see those *tits*?"

"See her reach out for your hand? Then she took *both* hands. . . ."

"Could you feel her tits against your chest? It looked like

you could. Did it make that little indented center of your palm itch for the push of her nipple against it? Did it?"

I didn't say much. Didn't have to. I was the *man*. Got a kiss from *that girl on the other train*.

"Hell, man. You could've *had* her . . . could've taken her to some motel there in Waycross and . . . *screwed* her. . . ."

Laughter. Speculation. Envy. Doubt. Wonder.

Later I stood outside on the landing between cars, watching the red clay embankments and pine trees roll by, less than an hour or so from the end of the line. One of the old black conductors came out and stood quietly beside me. He had the same straight back and gnarled hands as my old man. After a moment, without turning his gaze from the moving trees, he coughed quietly and said, "Listen, boy. Don't you worry 'bout what them other boys be sayin', 'bout what you could have done with that fine young lady." He shook his head slowly, let a wistful smile light up his aged mahogany face, and added, "Yessuh . . . that girl gave you a *moment*."

Soothsayer

A DAY or so before I finished Basic Training at Fort Benning, I sat in the shade of a Georgia pine with my Drill Instructor. He was a large muscular black man with a square face, a grim mouth, wide eyes, and flat ears pinned to the sides of his whitewalled head. He had a crisp, tailored uniform, a deep voice, and a fierce determination to transform teenage boys into soldiers. I do not remember his name, but he was representative of his breed. Anyone who has ever entered the armed services knows who I'm talking about, a solid professional career soldier dedicated to his craft, who never slept, never had so much as a wrinkle in his fatigues, and had at his immediate command a repertoire of blue language unparalleled in the history of verbal communication. He had come to me with the papers that announced I had been accepted to attend Officer's Candidate School. I did not know he had submitted my name.

"What's OCS, Sarge?" I asked with the confidence of a new soldier near the end of his initial training.

"It's where you leave the ranks of the great unwashed, boy," he answered in his sandpaper voice. "Where you become a gentleman and a leader so you can do less work for more pay."

"Sounds interesting, Sarge, but even a brand-new buck private like me knows it's the *sergeants* who actually run this army."

"You remember that and you'll be okay, boy. Thing is, they need bright and shiny faces to stand out in front of the formations, bright and shiny faces on the ground to turn and pass on the commands from those command choppers circling above you at great heights, bright and shiny faces to *lead*."

"That's it? I'll just be a bright and shiny face?"

"You'll be bright and shiny," he said, his eyes distant, "and you'll be killed a lot, you and the other bright and shiny ones, when you go to Vietnam."

New Blood

My jungle fatigues and boots were hopelessly new when I arrived at my first in-country assignment, a 155mm self-propelled artillery battery straddling Highway 19 between the Mang Yang Pass, and An Khe. I was a brand-new butter-bar second lieutenant, a blatant FNG (fucking new guy), and had my head stuck so far up my ass I couldn't even light a candle: not enough oxygen. The battery CO had already decided I'd be a forward observer because my FDC (fire direction center, where target coordinates, azimuth, and estimated distance were mathematically worked into elevation and powder charges for the guns to accurately place their rounds) skills were shaky. I was told to "hang around" until they figured out what to do with me.

A section of the highway ran right through the perimeter, and all day there'd be traffic on the road, trucks, tanks, Viet civilian vehicles, MP jeeps, all kicking up smoke and dust. It was an important and well-traveled road, rich in history. Both Pleiku and An Khe were major centers of commerce and communication for the Viets, and Pleiku was home for the Fourth Infantry Division, while An Khe held the 173rd Airborne Brigade. In between, only two klicks from where our battery was positioned, was the Mang Yang Pass, a place where many French soldiers had died in a classic Viet Minh ambush. Triple-strand wire gates in our perimeter were pulled open during the day, closed at night. Outside these gates sat the ubiquitous Coke girls with their coolers, half-naked kids, old men. The usual motley collection. Even after only a few days in-country they had already become part of the background scenery for me, always there.

I stood near my low bunker in the late afternoon, watched the hustle-bustle in our battery area, looked toward the road and saw no Coke girls or kids, and thought that odd. I watched an M-48 tank rumbling from my left to right toward An Khe, and saw the tank commander turn his head to the left as he stood in the cupola. A few yards beyond the tank there appeared a puff of greasy black smoke, and a second later I heard the grating *crump* of the explosion. I saw the exhaust from the tank as the driver gunned it even as the CO dropped inside and pulled the hatch closed. *Crump, crump:* two more greasy black puffs appeared closer to the road. I was running my sandpaper tongue around my parched mouth, trying to find enough spit to ask someone what was going on, when I heard the first yells of *"Mortars! Mortars! Incoming!"*

"Holy shit," I thought, "we're getting *hit*. The VC or NVA are nearby, actually dropping mortar rounds into a tube aimed at *me*. This is *wild*. I'm standing in the combat zone and we're getting *mortared*." My musings were interrupted when someone brushed past me in a run and yelled, "Get your bright new ass *down*, LT, we got incoming!" I turned to my left and dove into the first big sandbagged bunker I saw. It was a machine-gun bunker on the east side of the perimeter.

Three or four others huddled in the cool dampness, looking out the small firing port where the snout of the M-60 pointed. Now I could hear our 155s firing counterbattery fires, their tubes cranked almost straight up, low-powder charges behind the shells—this to send it up in a high arc that would bring it down close to our own perimeter. Close is where *he* would be.

"Wonder if we'll get a ground attack?" someone asked.

"Holy *shit*," said another voice, "it's *Joe*."

I turned to the entrance, and there crouched a young Hispanic soldier, his arms bloody, a frightened look on his face. Joe was one of the enlisted men (EM) who had been kind to me, showed me around. Now he leaned forward slowly and fell into my outstretched arms. I saw the blood on him, but could find no wounds.

"Hit," he said as he ran his fingers along his sides, "I'm hit . . . it's burning hot." Then he began to moan. I managed to lay him on a cot along one wall, ripped open his shirt, and found five tiny holes weeping blood on his right side, spaced within the rib cage.

I didn't know what to do.

The mortars could still be heard falling, *crunching*, ripping all through the perimeter, several times very close to our bunker. Behind them came the booms of our own guns firing out in an attempt to hit back and deter any ground attack. Over this came the sound of the M-60 in the bunker. I guessed it was being fired as a precaution, because so far there were no NVA charging in.

We had no first-aid kit. The compresses the guys had on their web gear seemed too big for Joe's wounds. But he was in pain, squirming on the cot, gritting his teeth, letting out a low moan occasionally. The blood continued to seep out of his chest, and even though I was an FNG, I understood slivers of shrapnel had pierced him, had cut their way in, had caused who knew what internal damage. Finally I looked at the five holes, the blood oozing out, and spread my fingers wide. I placed the tip of each finger and thumb on a hole and pressed. The pressure stopped the bleeding, and the feel of my touch somehow calmed Joe. He smiled at me and passed out.

I held my fingers on Joe for a long time, listening to the battle, wishing I could do more. Suddenly I was pushed aside by the medic as he tumbled into the bunker. He had heard about Joe and had run through the incoming to do his job. He pulled my hand away, gave Joe a quick once-over, and said to me gently, "I got it, LT. You did right."

"Hey, LT," said another voice as I turned away from the medic. "Fucking M-60's jammed, and we can *hear* the god-damned gook mortar tube out there."

I moved to the gun, lifted the feed cover, and pulled the cocking lever handle once or twice; a round clicked into place. I closed the cover and found myself with the gun shouldered, my eyes looking out the small firing port. I cocked my head to listen through all the other noise, and sure enough, I could hear the hollow *chung, chung* of their mortar being fired. *They* were out there, within *hearing*, firing their mortars at us. At *me*. Those little bastards. I listened, pictured the tube and its crew set up in a dry streambed a couple of hundred yards from me, and began firing the machine gun in that direction. I lifted the barrel slightly to get the rounds over the wire, and tried to will them to go where my mind's eye saw the enemy. The gun was warm and heavy, smelled like hot oil and gunpowder, and felt good bucking against my shoulder. One of the guys helped me feed and the medic turned long enough to say, "Get some, LT."

A few minutes later came the quiet, then the calls of "All clear." I stopped firing the gun, reluctant to let it go. I helped carry Joe out of the bunker to a dust-off that came for him. On the way the medic told me he thought Joe would make it okay. Somehow word got around the battery that I had helped Joe, had managed to get the M-60 going, had done good. Guys nodded and said hello later as I walked with the battery commander during damage assessment. I had arrived.

I looked at my hands and saw Joe's blood, dried to a coppery sheen. I didn't want to wash it off.

Journeyman

I WONDERED about my enemy in Vietnam. Who was he, what was he like, what were his dreams, his hopes, why did he want to kill me? Many men spent an entire tour in Vietnam without ever seeing a living enemy soldier. Dead ones, sure—twisted, sightless, openmouthed lumps of meat tangled in the wire, waxen in the first light of day. We would dig through their packs and find letters from home, some Tao or animist passage, the always rather formal photograph of a young woman or family, a small book of French poetry. It was difficult, however, to look at their dead forms and picture them as living beings, human, like us. When I returned to the green I took my varied memories of what we found in their packs, the exotic and sad sounds of their music, things I had heard about them, images of their brothers from the south, and molded them into the composite form of Tran.

The night sweated. The heat and dampness cloaked us in foggy gauze, sounds and sights were muted or intensified with a dark jungle's capriciousness. Into this mud, vegetation, loam, and tangle-tree sauna crept People's Soldier Tran, a regular private in the Army of North Vietnam. He crawled quietly on his belly, inching forward, letting his face and shoulders push aside the leaves and vines as he came to me. He stopped less than thirty feet from where I waited, having reached the end of his purposeful journey after three months on the move. With his left hand he gripped the stock of his Kalashnikov automatic rifle, the long pointed bayonet fixed at the end of the barrel. With his right he palmed a grenade, a potato-masher type known to us as a Chi-Com grenade even though many were produced in-country by faithful Freedom from Oppression People's Ordnance Workers. People's Soldier Tran had never thrown one of the grenades before this night, and had been issued it with only quick instructions a few hours after his arrival at the staging area less than a kilometer from where he lay.

Tran had left his home in the North those months ago with a heavy heart but a determined mind. At twenty, he was the oldest of three brothers; he worked a small farm with his family. The Glorious War Against the Tyrannic Americans had been raging for years, and many young men from his province had already traveled south. Tran had no doubt about the righteousness of his mission or the need for his participation, but he worried about his family and the farm. And he worried about Mai. She was sixteen years old, also from a farmer's family, a whisper of a girl with long shiny black hair, impossibly smooth skin, big watching eyes dark and deep like a forest pond, and a voice so sweet and pure he was seduced by it each time she spoke. Tran had held Mai's hand as they talked quietly the night he left, swept by a wave of melancholy from a song on her small radio, a song about a soldier who went off to war and the strong and fair maiden who promised to wait for him. Mai promised to wait. During the long and arduous journey south toward this night, her promise was the blood that flowed through Tran's heart.

The long march south on the Ho Chi Minh Trail, or the People's Victory Road, was not for the faint of heart or weak of body. With his own eyes Tran had seen the havoc and terror wreaked on his compatriots by the hated American jet bombers, felt the stunning confusion and fear caused by the sudden tearing explosions of artillery rounds that seemed to fall on them from nowhere. On more than one occasion he tried to bury himself in the heaving earth, his ears filled with the thunder of bombs and the screams of those torn apart by burning steel. He prayed. To what deity he prayed he was not sure. He knew of Buddha, of course, and of the Christ, too. Most of his family were animists, and they all worshipped their ancestors. He grew up surrounded by monks and schooled by missionaries, listened intently to all the teachings, and tried hard to put a name and face on what he really believed. He blamed himself for his failure and found some little contentment in the hope that there was *something* out there, some divine force he could petition in a hoarse babble as the night was torn by napalm and high explosives.

He had been tough and determined enough to survive the trip, had been trained and equipped along the way, had succumbed to the constant political indoctrination even as one accepts the air one breathes, and was now ready to do his part in an important battle against the drug-ridden, corrupt, politically retarded, slovenly, racist, and weak American soldiers. He waited in the blanket of darkness for the signal, other soldiers from his unit all around him. With the signal, he had been repeatedly instructed, pull the string at the bottom of the stick grenade to arm it, throw it at the Americans' position, then rise up and charge forward to shoot or bayonet any enemy soldier who survived the grenade's explosion.

I waited, too. My three-man forward observer team had been tagged on to an infantry platoon that afternoon. They needed someone to assist them in directing artillery fire, and I had been in and out of that area several times. We lay in hastily prepared positions, shallow foxholes with the high end facing where we knew the NVA would come. We knew they were there, in the night. One of the LPs had whispered, "Lots of movement coming all around us," into the radio, then had gone silent. My M-16 was locked and loaded, full magazines stacked on my rucksack by my left leg. My eyes were wide and staring, my mouth dry and slightly open, my breathing slow and steady. My Recon was to my left, my RTO to my right. We had already checked in on the artillery net and air support frequencies, and could bring down the steel on short notice. So we hung there in the green.

Tran heard the signal, felt a surge of crazy scary intoxicating strength, armed the hand grenade, rose, and threw it hard toward his enemy. Then he lunged to his feet, brought his AK-47 up across his chest, and ran forward with a high-pitched yell toward the place in the jungle night that would be torn open by the explosion of his grenade.

I watched the grenade come looping at us out of the green darkness and saw it land in the fresh dirt two feet behind me. In the split second after it hit and before the arming charge fired I instinctively shrugged my face behind my right shoulder in an effort to turn away from the searing shrapnel that would follow. But the grenade did not explode. It sparked yellow for one second, then farted out a desultory handful of white powder and lay there, stupid and inert. In that instant I turned back toward the jungle from where the grenade had come and saw the figure of a running NVA soldier coming toward us, shouldering through the foliage, rifle up, eyes shining in the gloom.

I gave him a burst of six on full automatic from about ten feet away. The rounds ripped him open from his crotch to his throat and punched him down and back into the mud and leaves, his legs kicking wildly. He was dead before he came to rest spread-eagled on his back, his milky eyes staring sightlessly at the high jungle canopy that was his shroud.

Hearts and Minds

I'D only been in-country a short time when I was assigned an RTO and Recon Sergeant and told to take my little outfit and occupy a daylight artillery OP (observation post) on top of the Mang Yang Pass, north side. Each morning we'd take the jeep down dusty Highway 19, early, before the engineers swept it for mines, drive right into the heart of the pass, and turn off into a small logging road. At that point the undulating green hardwood forest on the north and south side of the pass formed nearly vertical walls on our right and left, rising sheer up the mountains. The southeast section would still be in deep shadow, like the richer green of deep water; the northwest would already be lightening, more pale and dusty greens and silvers sweeping away and up toward our position. Even a puny little butterbar like me, sitting at the bottom of that pass surrounded by higher ground densely carpeted with perfect places to hide, was hit with an immediate sense of foreboding. Any French Mobile Armored Group that drove into that pass without first securing it from the top down should have just zipped themselves into bodybags before they left, saving the Viets the trouble. The place was the poster child of road ambush locations, okay?

But very beautiful. It was orderly hardwood forest, mahogany, teak, exotic far eastern giants different from what we have because even with their size and girth they still formed *jungle*. Strong tall trees reaching skyward, cathedral columns of trunks, sunlight streaming down to our faces through the stained-glass canopy of leaves above. Open on the ground, not scrubby and tangled, a place where sound carried and you whispered because of the majesty of it, not the fear. There were Viet woodcutters in there, too. You could smell that singular wet early-morning burning-firewood smell, hear the *whack*-pause, *whack*-pause of an ax being wielded a few feet or a few hundred yards away. We always suspected Viet woodcutters of being VC, of course, out there free and nonpolitical. I had the feeling they simply wanted to go about their business with no hassle from either side; they always waved when we passed and looked like basic workingmen to me, so who knew? We would wave back and continue the brutal climb toward the OP in our straining jeep, rifles out, eyes still puffy from sleep. We'd park the jeep near the crown behind where our OP was set, inside some old French bunkers, make radio contact with the batteries, fire up some coffee, and try to ease into the day.

The ARVN kept a platoon-size unit up on the pass. They had their women and children with them, had built little hootches of cardboard and corrugated tin backed up against caves dug into the crown, and there they held firm against the Communist tide that threatened to overwhelm them. They did this by making some sort of agreement with the local VC leaders. The agreement probably kept them from observing very much in the way of enemy movements through the area, but it kept them alive. They were coldly polite to us each morning. We were, after all, the big brother Americans with all the good war stuff to help them in their valiant fight against aggression. Stuff they could sell on the black market. So we would settle down for the day; they would go back to their lives, and the war was as close to us then as it was to the thousand dead Frenchmen who were supposedly buried standing up on the western slope of the mountain.

Late one afternoon, on top of the pass, my RTO squatted beside me as I swept the highway far below with my binos. He was pissed off.

"Fuckin' ARVNs took our C's, LT."

"The kids? So what? Let 'em have some."

"No way, it wasn't the kids . . . and they took the whole fucking case."

A case of C-rats contained twelve individual meals. Each meal box had little packets of gum and toilet paper and the ever valuable cigarettes. There were three of us, so a case was expected to last at least a couple of days. Being who we were, and having plenty, we were always handing packets and cans and boxes out to the kids . . . the ever-present Viet kids with their hand out in front of a knowing grin. But I have never liked a thief, and this just hit me wrong.

"They took the whole *case?*"

"Right off the back of the jeep, LT." Pause. "What should we do?"

"Have you asked around to the ARVN's?"

"Ain't nobody seen nothin'. Slopes just layin' in their hammocks laughin' at our ass."

"Okay."

I stalked over to the little enclave of ARVN hovels. Above me the hard hot sun speared down through the perfect unbroken sky. The dirt my boots kicked up from the OP area was almost as red as Georgia clay. I spotted the old noncom who was the leader of the ARVN's: no shiny officer with ascot and aviator sunglasses lived on this OP for the Viets. He was small, wiry; late forties, I'd guess. His black hair was cut to stubble on his head and chin, his skin was dark and dry, his hands rough and dirty. He wore green utilities with the shirt untucked, and yellow shower shoes. He had a pug nose, bad teeth, and watery eyes. He had a watch on each wrist, and one pinned to his shirt. I gestured angrily at my jeep, then at the ARVN.

"Where are my C's, pal? Where are my C's?"

He looked at me and blinked.

"From our jeep. One of your people took a case of C-rations off the back of our jeep. Where the hell are they?"

The guy shrugged. The Viet can shrug just like a French-man, and it pissed me off. I shouldered past him and bent into one of the makeshift hootches. I took inventory. The usual smells of rotting fruit, wet firewood, and nuoc mam sauce, one-each toothless old woman, one-each chubby young woman with far-east Gerber baby sucking away on a nipple. Blank faces. No C-rats. I grunted and backed out. Went to the next one, then the next, scowling, pulling at hammocks, clothing, boxes. No rats. Went into one hootch and there was a nice fat C-ration box at the base of some makeshift shelves. I reached for it and the one-each toothless old woman began shaking her head and clucking and clucking and hissing. I pulled the box and most of the wall and shelf buckled and collapsed onto the dirt floor, candles, cooking utensils, and old fruit cans flying. The box was old and empty. The woman glared at me, silent.

I only grew angrier, and was beginning to draw a crowd. Seems the valiant ARVN didn't like me charging around in their homes without a warrant. They had their M-1's, and they stared at me sullenly. It was our understanding that none of them spoke English, and we had only a few words of Viet. I resorted to volume, inflection, and demeanor to communicate. I addressed the old ARVN noncom, but it was for them all.

It just rubbed me wrong, you know? We were there to *help* these people, we were brothers-in-arms against a common enemy, right? Brothers-in-arms can trust each other. Now I see that much of my anger stemmed from disappointment. I wanted to be on the side of right, and good, and I wanted the Viets of the south—the ones I fought beside—to be good and decent in my eyes, to act properly.

"I want those goddamned C-rations one of you sorry sons of bitches took off my jeep. I don't give a fuck if I have to tear down every one of these shacks, I don't care if I have to drop a grenade into every piece-of-shit bunker, and I don't care if I have to call six batteries of my own friggin' artillery down onto the top of this crappy hill. Understand?" Then, after a couple of deep breaths, I added quietly, "You want C's, we'll get you some, but don't take 'em off my jeep without asking."

No one moved. No one responded. After maybe thirty seconds my recon, who stood behind me with his M-16 leveled at the ARVN noncom, spit and said, "Sure got a way with words, Lieutenant."

Then a young boy, ten years or so, stepped forward and beckoned. I followed him around to the other side of the crowd to a small opening that led to a bunker. It was not furnished or equipped, just dirt walls and floor. Lying on the ground against the far wall was the case of C's, apparently unopened. I hesitated, thinking booby trap, and the kid brushed past me and picked it up. No boom. He handed it to me and walked out.

Back on the OP I found everyone holding their positions,

same sullen looks, same M-1's, same searing sun. I dropped the case at the feet of the old ARVN, knelt, ripped it open, and stepped back.

"Tell your people," I said as I gestured, "they can take what they want. You want C's? I'll get 'em for you, okay? But don't just *take* 'em."

He looked down at the box, shrugged his Gallic shrug, and walked away. The rest of the Viets followed suit.

We skedaddled before dark, like we always did, wind ripping through the rocky jeep as we careened down the logging road toward the bottom of the pass. Recon drove, I sat shotgun, RTO in back. RTO leaned forward, his head between ours, and said, "There it is, Lieutenant."

"There is what?"

"There is this motherfucking Veetnam. . . ."

"How?"

"We got more fucking C-rats and shit than anybody could eat in three lifetimes, LT. We ain't gonna sell 'em, and ain't nobody can *take* them from us. We want to *give* 'em away."

"Yeah?"

"Fuckin' gooks, *our* gooks, they can have our C-rats and all our other shit six ways from Sunday, but it don't mean a goddamned thing to them unless they *steal* 'em from us."

"There it is."

And we were out of the crosshairs of the pass, and northbound on the highway.

Cherry

WITH the fingers of her right hand she formed a circle. She penetrated the circle with the rigid index finger of her left hand and smiled at me as she moved the finger in and out. It was a classic gesture, and she left no room for doubt as she tilted her head and raised an eyebrow in query. She was tall for a Viet, willowy and smooth with a perfect eggshell complexion, long straight shiny black hair, an oval face, and the cat's eyes of a mythical Oriental princess. She was older than twelve but younger than twenty, I think, and stood lovely before me dressed in simple light pajamas and thong sandals. The sun had only been with us for a little while, and the morning ground fog misted everything and diffused the edges of objects more than a few yards away. She had come out of the mist on the narrow road in silence, her graceful walk accented by the secret and bemused expression on her face.

I stood stunned and awkward in her questioning gaze, dressed for war and prepared for it. I had been in-country several months, was not green by any means, and talked the talk and walked the walk of a young veteran quite comfortable in his warrior skin. I had not had much contact with the females of Vietnam, though, except for the women and children of the villages I swept through searching and destroying. They were only women and children to me, and the code I'd brought with me from home, despite the propaganda and even despite things I had seen with my own eyes, made them noncombatants. I was a combatant, as was the enemy I sought, so the women and children of the villages were just . . . there. I had spent very little time in base camp, and almost none in the bigger towns or Saigon. Of course I had seen the whores, had watched my men dally with them, had politely declined my men's offer of a paid ride. To their open amusement, I'd declined more than once. I was as experienced with women as any American teenage boy when I came to the war, more talk than actual time at the controls. My men respected me as their young leader, fought beside me, and cared for me, but they razzed me nonetheless about my war-zone virginity.

She stood there inviting me, and I hesitated. I became aware of how acutely *aware* I was of her, the nearness, the scent, the physical warmth of her. But hell, I stood hugged by my gear, armed and primed and locked and loaded. Besides, this was a war, not a sock hop, and *they* were out there in the jungle representing the dark side and carrying their weapons, and we would be shoving off soon to find them, and kill them. My men sprawled around me on both sides of the road, watching, grinning. They saw my hesitation, and several shook their heads in disbelief. Finally my Recon helped me make the decision with a gentle shove.

"We got time, Lieutenant," he said quietly as he knelt a few feet away.

"Yeah, but . . . hell, we're out here in the middle of . . ."

"She is fucking *primo*, LT. A bed of grass under a canopy of leaves beats the dog shit out of some crappy room in downtown Pleiku anytime. My gut feeling is she don't do this too often and is kinda takin' a chance herself. And we got plenty of time before this bogart piece-of-shit poor excuse of an operation moves out."

"But, sarge . . . I mean, all the guys will know I took her and did it, and . . . I don't think it will look right."

"Just *do* it, LT, before one of these guys you're so worried about grabs her ass, pulls her into some bushes, and bangs the hell out of her himself. Shit, might be *me*, Lieutenant. I mean, that is absolutely one of the finest-lookin' gook cunts I have seen since I been here in this fucking toilet bowl." He shook his head in wonder, and added quietly, "That is one fucking primo piece of Viet pussy—and you the one tellin' me you wanted to come to this war to experience war, to live this part of life in this time of your life because this is our war and might be your only chance and war is part of life and you want to learn all about life in its entirety and all that other philosophical bullshit. So here comes a slice for you. Go experience it."

I should have felt vulnerable lying naked in the grass with her, but I didn't. I felt like a man as I looked at her face and body beneath mine, the taste of her spicy and exotic on my lips, the feel of her electric on my fingertips. She spoke to me, her breath running hot across my skin, her words made intoxicating by the strange language and tone of her voice. As she arched her back and cried out to me I felt her fingers grip the muscles in my shoulders, and I was lost.

The warm damp smell of the surrounding jungle, and *her*, gently invaded my senses and brought me back, and she laughed quietly and watched my face as she stroked my lips with her fingers. She spoke, knowing the words meant nothing to me, and I bathed in the things she said. After a few minutes she pulled away and sat up. When she reached for her discarded clothing I knew our brief sojourn was ending. She sat on her haunches and watched as I dressed, until I stood before her once more the soldier. Bumbling now, I reached into my pocket for cash, but she stepped close, smiled, grabbed my wrist, and shook her head. Confused, I waited. She pulled my hand out of my pocket, held it in hers, and with the fingers of her other hand touched my clunky high school ring.

Two days after my time with the girl I was bleeding slightly from two small cuts on my face, scared, and running like hell across the edge of a sun-seared clearing at the foot of the jungle. My Recon ran beside me, my RTO beside him. We had broken off from the main part of the unit, which had been pinned down in a ravine after tripping a ragged ambush. I was angry because we had warned the unit's leader that their intended route of march took them through perfect ambush country, and sure as hell it had exploded in our faces in the heat of the afternoon and guys went down and the jungle was filled with screams and curses. To sit was to die, I knew, so we broke out to the right where their fire seemed to trickle off, guessing that would be their escape. We had a low ridgeline as our goal, had exchanged bursts of fire twice already with others moving that way, and were looking for a fight and the high ground at the same time.

I saw them first, two enemy soldiers running around the edge of a large clump of scrub trees. They wore the khaki-and-green uniform of the NVA, rucksacks, and pith helmets, and they cradled AK-47's in their arms. Their eyes shone bright in the shadows of their helmets, and even from fifty feet I saw those eyes clearly as they widened in surprise. I slashed my M-16 off my hip and fired two quick bursts of six as I ran. The rounds caught the enemy soldiers at gut level and they writhed and tumbled, their arms flailing as they rag-dolled into the ground.

"*Fuck!*" yelled my Recon, and we kept running for the ridgeline.

One hour later, after the medevac choppers, after the radio reports, after the regrouping, we went back. I wanted to see if the bodies were still there, as so often they simply disappeared, and I wanted to see what they carried in their packs. They waited, twisted and sprawled in the heat and flies, shattered, bloodied, and gray. My Recon studied them carefully, looking for signs of booby traps, then grabbed each one by a wrist and pulled until they lay flat on their backs, dead eyes staring at the hard blue sky around us.

"Fuckin' gook females, Lieutenant," said the Recon.

"Biggerin' shit," said the RTO.

I bent closer, holding my breath. One was chunky, with short black hair and a square face with sharp little teeth. My RTO had already grabbed her pack and was rifling through it as Recon picked up their weapons. I looked at the other. She was tall for a Viet, willowy and smooth with a perfect eggshell complexion, long straight shiny black hair, an oval face, and the cat's eyes of a mythical Oriental princess. She was older than twelve, but less than twenty, I think, but it didn't matter now anyway and those eyes were flat, dull, rubbery, and her pale lips stretched across her teeth and slightly protruding purple-blue tongue. I grabbed her pack and quickly emptied it onto the ground. I tossed through the extra set of clothing, the papers, the small knife and can of fruit. I threw it aside and reached for her, tearing at her uniform, shoving my fingers into the pockets, pulling at her fingers, ripping the blouse to see if anything hung around her neck. She yielded to my assault without resistance, her body loose and uncaring in my hands.

"What the fuck you doin', LT?" asked my Recon.

"Is it *her*, Sarge?" I whispered.

"What?"

"The one from the other day—the one on the road . . . the one I . . ."

Recon leaned close and slowly examined the dead face. After a long moment he pulled back. "Fuck, I can't tell, LT," he said. "This is a dead fucking gook, and that one on the road was one fine piece of woman." He looked at me and shrugged. "Who the fuck knows, you know?"

I stared at him, then searched her again. Finding nothing I continued to kneel beside her, examining what she had become.

"What the fuck you lookin' for, Lieutenant?"

Before I could answer we heard a yell from the tree line and some of the guys from the unit came out of the shadows and stood at the edge of the clearing. "Hey! We're movin' out!" one of them yelled.

"Let's go, LT," said Recon.

"You guys find anything interesting on those two dinks?" yelled the other soldier.

"Nah . . . just their AK's," answered my RTO.

"Well, listen to this!" yelled the soldier. "One of the ones we wasted back at the ambush site had somebody's high school ring on him. Can you believe it? Had it tied around his neck on a piece of leather. Is that weird, or *what*? Fucking NVA dink with a high school ring from the World?"

"He still got it?" asked my sergeant as he gave me a strange look.

"Hell no, he ain't still got it," answered the other guy. "He ain't got no dick and no ears either. We took that ring and gave it to the captain, and he took it with him outta here on the fuckin' chopper."

I stared at the soldier, then down at the dead girl at my feet.

"Let's get the fuck outta here, Lieutenant," said the sergeant quietly as he turned to go.

I left the clearing behind the others, and soon the warm damp smell of the jungle enveloped me.

Listening Post

SOMETIMES things aren't what they seem. The vegetation wasn't really triple canopy, but sparse double going to triple as it climbed into a part of the Central Highlands. Green, strong, and fragrant, with plenty of scrub down low. All the ambush possibilities made travel slow. It didn't have the cathedrallike serenity of honest triple canopy. It wasn't really evening, either, not that there is much of evening in the deep, misty forest-jungle of the highlands. You have late afternoon, you begin to settle into a position, and then it's *nighttime*, baby. And it wasn't really my unit. An infantry platoon of the 173rd Airborne, with a lieutenant choppered out after twisting his ankle, leaderless in the eyes of some captain on the other end of the radio, and me a forward observer type shuffling from one unit to another like some poor relative. Me, a lieutenant too, in-country three months, trained to *lead*, by God. So for that night I was the LT.

I *was* the LT, and I was checking with the real leaders of the platoon about the placement of the LP's. LP equals listening post, usually three unlucky men, sometimes two, maybe five, sent out from the platoon's perimeter to set up quietly and listen. The LPs might be a hundred meters from the perimeter, much less if it was thick country. Out there in the night with a PRC-25 radio, locked and loaded, mouths dry, eyeballs straining, they peered into the green mist, listening to the sweating foliage, waiting for some sign of *them*. The enemy liked to come in the night, and the LP's were out there to give warning.

Most nights in Vietnam went long, hot, and quiet, and the LP's were rewarded with morning after fighting their own imaginations through the dark hours. They'd stumble back into the perimeter with cotton teeth, bleeding eyes, and aching joints. Some nights brought reality to the nightmares—*they* came, and those on the other end of the radio would hear the hoarse whispers, the guttural calls for illumination, the far-off hollow booms of claymores ripping loose through the green. Then often, nothing more, nothing . . . and in the morning, nothing.

So I was the LT, checking the placement of my LP's.

"Where's number three, Sarge?"

"Straight out from here, LT . . . 'bout seventy meters maybe. Comin' up this way earlier we noticed a little draw bottomed with a dry streambed. Looked like a good approach to this fuckin' piece-of-shit real estate we're rentin' for the night."

"Yeah, this is not the *best* position on this side of the mountain."

"I didn't pick it, LT."

"Okay, so you've got three LP's, and this is number three. Who's on the team out there?"

"Beast."

I looked at him and waited, just a second looie, shave-tail, butterbar, shit-assed LT . . . but too tired to be fucked with.

"Beast, LT. A guy everybody in the platoon, actually the whole damned company calls Beast. He's got a regular name, you know, but he's extremely, totally, and magnificently bad. A wonderfully insane second-tour kind of grunt who I guess *likes* this scene. Veet-fucking-nam, body counts, night ambushes, napalm, the whole fucking ménage-à-toilet . . . understand?"

"He's a mentally ill cartoon character, Sergeant?"

"Nah, LT. It's kinda hard to explain. He's a big guy, sunburned alla time, peaceful blue eyes lookin' off to who the fuck knows where. Sleepy-lookin', you know? But hard, hard and quiet and . . . I'll tell ya what, LT. Back at base camp—whenever *this* whore of an outfit ever *gets* to base camp—back at base camp the fucking blacks leave him *all* the fuck alone. Understand?"

"Okay, Sarge. This guy Beast is mental, tough, and respected. I guess I'm glad he's with *us*. So who's out there with him tonight on LP number three?"

"Just the Beast, sir. He does LP's all alone—"

"C'mon. No way you can—"

"Look, Lieutenant, that's what we got in this sorry-assed outfit. Beast does LP's alone, and we let him, okay?"

There was still enough light to make out the different trees when I eased out of the perimeter and made my way through the draw bottomed by the dry streambed. I'd had the RTO tell LP number three, "Two-niner coming to you." The radio static was broken twice in reply. I moved carefully and quietly, looking for his broad back or a sign of his gear, and almost crawled right past him in the gloom.

"What in the fuck are you doin', LT?" he asked in a raspy voice. It was a polite query, not a challenge. I answered in kind.

"I'm the LT of your platoon for the night, checking up on one of my men who's sitting an LP by himself."

"What'd you do, *listen* to all that crap they taught you at West Point?"

"I'm just an OCS kind of lieutenant, not a ring-knocker, and I guess I had to see you for myself."

He stared at me a moment, then turned his big head and watching eyes to the encroaching blackened green. I felt compelled to press on.

"Look, soldier—"

"Most of the guys call me Beast, sir."

"Look, Beast. Your sarge told me you are tough and experienced and comfortable out here, but *I'm* not comfortable with you being out here alone. I'm the LT, I'm responsible, and I'm sending out another couple of troops to be with you."

"No, LT. I do these alone."

"No? You tell me no?"

I heard a chopper, not too close. It was that pulsing, drumming, heartwarming sound of the good old Huey, lifting off and climbing out from an LZ within a klick of us. The platoon I was with was part of a battalion-sized operation that had had scattered contacts all through the previous two days. We were roughly in the center of all the units and actions in the area. The sound of Hueys coming and going became a kind of white noise in the green, always there. It was a good sound mostly, strong, comforting: choppers, Hueys. *Ours.* They brought us there, sure, but they brought us food, too, and mail, and they took us out when we were wounded, and they took us home when it was time. I cocked my head to listen as the helicopter clawed up into the pale sky, unseen.

"Takin' out wounded, maybe," said the Beast quietly. "Or gook prisoners, or both." He spit.

"How about if *I* stay out here with you tonight?" I asked, surprising even myself.

He laid his broad forehead gently onto the receiver group of his M-16, and said quietly, "Lieutenant, with all due respect: Get the fuck outta here." Then he looked up.

I heard it, too, and joined him in staring up through the foliage and reaching tree branches, up toward the closing sky, toward the sound. It was a keening, very high-pitched and wavering, and it cut across the deeper sound of the fading helicopter. It came from up there, though, where the chopper was. As it grew louder it deepened in richness and intensity. The sound amplified its way down through the jungle around us, toward us, enveloping us. I realized it was a scream, a long wailing helpless hopeless angry terror-stricken scream which pierced LP number three, the jungle, the Central Highlands, Veet-fucking-nam, and my soul.

I glanced at Beast. His head was tilted back slightly, his eyes wide, his mouth compressed into a slit. He waited.

With a *thump*, the scream ended. We heard a leafy crash, then another, one more, then what sounded like "*Oh*." After a final snapping sound, not ten feet in front of us a man's body plunged to a tearing stop on a broken tree stump. With the end of the fall, the end of the scream, the end of the broken branches, came an eerie and immediate silence. Not even the chopper sounds lingered, and my already violated ears sought something more. But there was no more. Only the silence of the jungle as evening falls to night, and the body of a Viet soldier stabbed and twisted on the broken tree stump. Looked like an actual NVA soldier, not a local VC. Had green cloth trousers down around his ankles. Had Ho Chi Minh racing slicks on his feet. Had a green cloth long-sleeved shirt with small red tabs on the collar. Had his hands duct-taped behind his back. Had his mouth stretched so wide open his upper teeth showed clearly in the gloom. His chest had burst. Broken ribs clutched at the tree stump like the fingers of a pale skeletal hand.

He had come writhing out of the evening sky, his body still accelerating as it discovered our listening post. A short chopper ride to altitude, then a forced lesson in the effects of gravity on politics.

The world around the impaled body rushed back to me, and I gasped for air and fought the urge to vomit at the same time. My eyes ached, and my shaking hands felt like lead on my Car-15. I swallowed hard, gulped some loam-spiced mist, and forced myself to stop trembling. After what seemed like several minutes I slowly turned my head to look at Beast. He let his sleepy eyes meet mine for a moment, then he turned his gaze back to the nighttime jungle and the dead NVA soldier. He spit, and said, "He musta been a bad liar, huh, LT?"

I crawled back to safety inside the platoon's perimeter, and found the sergeant's hole after stumbling around for a few minutes accompanied by muted curses.

"What the fuck was the scream, LT?" he asked as he handed me a small metal flask that brought a pleasing fire to my gut. "Everybody on the perimeter thought they heard some kinda scream."

"It's raining gooks, Sarge," was my reply.

"Oh," he said. Then, "What about Beast?"

"Beast does LP's alone," I answered.

Eulogy

"**C**'MON, *c'mon c'mon* . . . it's comin' *in* . . . comin' in right *here*."

"*Shit*, we're in the shit, we're in the motherfuckin' *zone*. They got us dead to rights. We got to hunker *down*, got to get down out of it now."

"*Fuck you* get down. Get down and *die*, we got to shoot, we got to *move*. Shoot their sorry ass, shoot their ass, *shoot their ass*."

"Left is weaker, the *left*, the left is weaker. Trailin' off to the left. Watch my tracer, watch . . . watch!"

"Noooo. *No!* It's too motherfuckin' *much*. It's comin' down on us, we got to get *down*."

"Get down and die, fuckstick . . . get down and *die*."

"Motherfucker."

"Motherfucker."

"*Shoot the motherfuckers*. Shoot, shoot, shoot, shoot."

"Who the *fuck* tried to throw a grenade in this shit? Stupid son of a bitch. You think you're killin' dinks throwing a goddamned grenade so it bounces out of the vines and lands on *my* ass?"

"Well, did it go *off*, you fucking whiner?"

"No it didn't go off, asshole. You didn't pull the motherfuckin' piece-of-shit scum-sucking *pin*."

"*Shoot*. Shoot. Shoot. Shoot. Move left, move *left*. Get your sorry asses moving *left*, goddammit."

"Fuck *you*, move left. I'm just layin' here suckin' the mud outta this trail. You see the shit they're throwin'? You see the green tracer? Fuck *you*, move left."

"Well *shoot* them, poster child. What the fuck you here for?"

"I *am* shootin'. I'm just shootin' from *here*, okay?"

"Heads *down*, ARTY rounds comin' in. Our steel comin' down—"

"Move left, *left* goddammit."

"Heads down? I'm *already* eatin' out Mother Earth. How the fuck I'm s'posed to move left *and* keep my head down *and* shoot the motherfuckers, motherfucker? Ooooh, *man*, lookit that fuckin' artillery eat up that tree line, ooooh, *yeah*. Do it *again*, do it some *more*. *Eat that you gook cunts*."

"How you got so much breath to be screamin' at them when you so busy eatin' out Mother Earth? Don't scream at 'em, *shoot* at 'em."

"*Fuck you*. I'm eatin' and I'm shootin' and I'm screamin' and I'm movin' left and we are *kicking fucking ass*. You see it? Look at that dink stumblin' outta the trees, man. Lookit that silly motherfucker tryin' to run. *Holy shit*—you see how his little dink legs kept on runnin' after that artillery round blew him in *half*? Fuck, we *got* these shitheads, man. We got 'em, we got 'em."

"Keep shootin', shoot, shoot, shoot."

"Christ almighty, who's got some ammo?"

"*Ammo up, ammo up—*"

"Hey clusterfuck. Get your head outta the mud and look around. We're standin' up, we're standin' up and walkin' around and everything. This little bend-in-the-trail episode is *history*, man . . . and we standin' here."

"I knew that, man, I knew that."

"We fucked up a bunch of dinks, man, a *bunch* of dinks. They sittin' dead. Fuckin' dead in their holes, the mother-fuckers, still starin' down this sorry trail. The ones over in the tree line are *all* fucked up, man. We killed a lot of gooks on this one. They sprung it too soon, *before we were really in*."

"Who'd we lose?"

"Point. We lost Point. First burst took out his guts, then they ripped open his ass and the back of his head when he tried to crawl to the lieutenant."

"That's *it*?"

"Point. We lost Point. You know he played ball in college? Had an old Chevy. Worked part-time for a construction out-fit. His old man wanted him to stay in school and then go into his carpet business or somethin'."

"Yeah—he liked that Beach Boys song about the surfer girl, even though he was from the Midwest. Told me he got real drunk one night back home, and woke up the next morn-ing on the front lawn of the biggest church in town. Said his mom was pissed about it, but his old man thought it was funny. Said he didn't need to smoke dope to act dumb, could do it all by himself."

"He was sayin' he might go back to school when he got back to the World. Talked about bein' a teacher, maybe . . ."

"He got six stitches over one eye once stickin' up for some waitress who was bein' hassled by a bunch of bikers."

"Had a picture of his girl, topless on some beach. Fine."

"Loaned me twenty bucks before we shipped over here, and never hassled me for it back. Said he thought a lot of the countryside here was pretty. Said he liked to walk point."

"We fucked up a *bunch* of gooks, man."

"All we lost was Point."

"She was topless in the picture?"

"Smilin' into the camera for him. *Fine*."

"Shit."

"We lost Point."

Fire for Effect

You exist. Then you don't. You breathe, sweat, dream, curse, put one foot in front of the other as you walk into the green. Then you don't. You are alive with the other soldiers, pulling the same humid air into laboring lungs, your body whole, your mind either numb from fatigue or busy trying to work this whole thing out. Then, in the literal blink of an eye, a small piece of metal traveling at great speed comes out of the green and enters the living you . . . and you are gone. Just like that.

Just another walk in the sun.
Just another lousy day in paradise.
Another troop movement, company-size, platoons stretched out through the scrub, the clearings, the low hills and clutching jungle. Hot, clear, a little breeze; every grunt on the hike had seen worse days. We were moving from one Objective to another Objective with the loose orders to seek out and destroy the enemy along the way. Most of the grunts were

relaxed because there *were* no enemies. The day just didn't have that feel, no hot intel warning about VC or NVA movements, no recent contacts, no probes in the wire, not even any lobbed mortar rounds last night.

Everyone agreed that the countryside was often very pretty, though permeated with all those strange and mysterious Far Eastern smells. The line of green and brown pulled and bumped along, stopping now and then so a young platoon leader could say something on the radio to an impatient captain. The grunts were maintaining pretty good noise and spacing discipline for a regular U.S. line outfit, no radios blaring music, no loud conversations, no cigarettes unless flopped around on break. What we saw and felt was regulation G.I. issue Vietnam style: green towels draped over red sweaty necks or black creased sweaty necks, packs pulling into shoulder muscles, feet hot and spongy in damp socks, insect-repellent bottles tucked into helmet cover bands next to four-inch compresses. Helmet graffiti expounding the usual: "F.T.A."; "YEA THO I WALK THROUGH THE VALLEY OF DEATH I FEAR NO EVIL FOR I AM THE BADDEST MOTHERFUCKER IN THE VALLEY"; "JODY CAN HAVE HER"; "WHAT ARE *YOU* LOOKIN' AT?"; "SHORT-TIMER WITH ATTITUDE": brave words worn by guys no braver than the rest, but still putting one foot in front of the other. Cradled M-16's, M-60's, M-79's, here and there a LAAW, beaucoup grenades, ammo pouches, canteens. The jungle-bumble step toward the next Objective.

I was the FO attached to the line company of the Fourth Infantry for a couple of days, a red-leg kind of LT working with my RTO and Recon. We knew some of the grunts and a couple of the older NCO's from working with this outfit before, but all the officers were new. We did that to ourselves, of course. While our enemy had leaders who had been making war for years—they were in for the duration—we rotated our officers in and out of combat assignments. Actual combat time, leading platoon or company-size operations on the ground, is an important ingredient in the seasoning of any officer desiring promotion. We made sure our officers "got their tickets punched." An infantry lieutenant or captain might be on the ground, with a fighting unit, for six months, just enough time and experience to make him effective, then he'd be assigned somewhere up the line so another lieutenant or captain could take his shot at it. This guaranteed we'd have new, inexperienced people at the helm.

Distance does funny things to the sound of a bullet being fired at you. First you sense, then hear, the buzz, snap, whisper, or slap of the bullet whizzing past your head. A millisecond later you hear the flat report of the rifle that fired it, off in the tree line.

"*Incoming.*"

"Sniper! Sniper! *Get down.*"

"Didn't have to say that, LT, we're already down."

"Anybody see where he is? Where's that fire coming from? Get some fire out there, get some, get some—"

The entire lead platoon of the company was down in the bushes, some guys with their face in the dirt, some hugging the legs of the man in front of them, some kissing the forestock of their M-16, some trying to look up through the low foliage to spot their attacker. Heads were seriously *down*, though. With all the bad shit that could happen to a guy in that place, nobody wanted to get zipped into a bag for the Graves and Registration Unit because of a stupid *sniper.* The young LT platoon leader was right on it, having seen this *exact* scenario played out in Fort Benning, Georgia. He was on the radio to the impatient captain who waited with the other platoons; he was yelling at his platoon sergeant who yelled at his squad leaders. The LT wanted to fire and maneuver; he wanted one squad to lay down a base of fire toward the sniper while another squad flanked the location and got close enough to blow him out of there.

Zing . . . pow. "Son of a bitch is still shooting at us! Let's *move*, get some, get some."

It was always a very weird sensation to know someone—one of *them*—some *person* was shooting a gun at *you*. Never mind all the other grunts strewn around in the grass. That little bastard was aiming at *you*, and it made for a dry mouth, small-of-the-back wiggles, and not a small amount of anger.

The tree the sniper had chosen was a very attractive representative of its family, with a straight tall trunk, symmetrical branches reaching out in even lengths, and densely packed leaves forming a full canopy. He could sit high up in there, where we could not see him easily . . . yet he could see out through those leaves as he sighted his weapon. The tree was fronted by a clearing, which gave him a good view of anyone closing in, and it was backed by rising jungle where he could make his escape after shooting one or two of us.

The pastoral setting, the peaceful day, the nice walk and pleasant company made me feel awkward as I yelled to get the platoon leader's attention, like I didn't want to be *rude*. Finally he stopped yelling into his radio and at his platoon sergeant and looked at me with big eyes and open mouth.

"*What?*"

"Just wanted to remind you, Lieutenant," I said with a grin, "that you are not a *Marine* platoon leader."

"What the hell's that supposed to mean? We gotta goddamned sniper bringing fire onto us, and—"

"I know, but I mean the Marines have that 'economy-of-fire' thing and all, artillery not havin' enough rounds to waste 'em, platoon leaders aware of how careful they should be with the use of redleg."

"*Christ*. He fired *again*. Why the hell are you telling me this about the *Marines*? I got to get my teams moving against this friggin' sniper—"

"I'm your artillery, Lieutenant. Use me."

"Huh?"

"Isn't the captain already on your ass about takin' so long, the whole company movement held up while we deal with one sorry dink sniper?"

"Yeah."

"I'm the *firepower*. I've got the artillery, the gunships, the fast-movers, all the heavy steel at my fingertips. *Use* me."

He blinked. "Okay. Go ahead."

An artillery spotter's job was to call for supporting fire for the lightly armed infantry troops when they engaged their enemy. Many klicks away from the battle, the guns would fire at my request. I would try to see or hear the first round fall, and adjust from that, over . . . under, until the target was bracketed by explosions. At that point I could call for all the guns to bear, and the impact and power of the concentrated fire would often have a dramatic effect on the immediate situation. My RTO already had a battery of 155's up and humming. Recon had the grid coordinates, had given them to the RTO, used his compass to shoot an azimuth, had his binos locked on the tree. RTO grinned as he handed me the handset for the radio.

"Fire mission," I said quietly.

Several klicks away a guy in the 155 FDC took my info; he passed it to the gun-bunnies serving the six trailed guns, and they were readied.

Zing . . . pow.

I had the battery fire one smoke round for adjustment. We heard it, then saw a billow not far behind the tree. The grunts were sprawled in the grass around us, the two fire teams waiting. No one was hurt, the sun shone, the breeze blew, curious insects buzzed nearby.

Zing . . . pow.

He was up there in his tree. Probably a local VC type. Maybe he had a new SKS rifle they gave him, some ammo. Told him to go out and kill an American for Uncle Ho. Slow the invading Americans down, hurt them, make them think about how this land will never come under their control, how the people will fight. He listened, he took the rifle, he made his choice to make war that day.

Some of our troops were firing, sparingly, toward the tree, just to keep him in place. I'm sure the smoke round exploding into the jungle to his rear meant nothing to him.

"Drop seven-oh, request mixed HE with VT."—high explosive rounds, some of which would explode before hitting the ground, air bursts, tree trimmers. *"Fire for effect."* The entire six-gun battery of 155's would now fire at the exact spot in Vietnam where the brave sniper had decided to fight his war. "Shot, over." "Shot, out."

We waited.

With a booming, crunching, jarring roar, the tree and its surroundings were suddenly enveloped in a greasy black thunderstorm of fire, the ground and air bursts exploding in ragged breathtaking punches, red-orange centers flaming out followed by smoke, dust, mixed debris flying up, out, and away. The booms rolled across us and beyond like a buffeting wave.

"Get some!"

"Sounds like they're playing our song!"

"Fuckin' A . . . that was numbah *one!*"

"Suck on that, Charlie."

"*Saddle up.* Let's move out."

The two lead squads moved forward quickly but cautiously, and soon we were across the clearing and into the area of the sniper's tree. Someone passed back a shard of wood that had probably been part of a rifle stock. We were quiet as we moved through. The whole area was quiet. No more sniper fire. The tree was reduced to a blackened and bent trunk with a few stripped branches curving down instead of up. A few stubborn leaves clung to them. The sniper held his ground, wedged against the trunk, his feet resting in the crook of a strong branch. His feet were wrapped in sandals, his legs clothed in green trousers of heavy fabric. He had no shirt, and as I stood beneath him for a moment I saw he had an outie for a navel. From his navel up he was in disrepair, his chest blown open, his neck a blackened nub. What I think was his jaw lay on top of the nub; the rest of his face and skull were gone. He had no shoulders or arms. The sniper had become an obscene thing wedged into the remains of his obscene tree, surrounded by a blackened and torn wasteland as flayed as his skin.

The platoon leader walked beside me as we continued our mission, and said with a nod, "I can appreciate the idea of not endangering the lives of my troops when we have that firepower available, two-niner. And I'm sure you're aware of that very *Oriental* axiom which states, 'A lion uses all of its strength even when attacking a rabbit' . . . but I still would have liked to work a little fire-and-maneuver on him."

Before I could answer his old platoon sergeant spit and said with a hard laugh, "Don't overanalyze it, Lieutenant. I don't know if there's a Vietnamese word for Bushido, but maybe that guy in the tree thought he had it. Either way, he was a stupid dink sniper who brought a *rifle* to an artillery battle."

Army Issue

To look at a dead gook (in an atmosphere of war in a faraway land it is easy to dehumanize your enemy: gook, dink, slope; they were different from us, and somehow less, so they had less impact in death) was one thing. To look at a dead American was a completely different head trip. You looked at yourself when you saw the body of a man who had humped the boonies with you, eaten the crappy C-rats with you, told stories of home with you. You looked at death, and turned away, but your mind wouldn't let it go, even as your heart tried to bury it deep. When the questions came, they were the big ones: Who are we? What are we? What in the living hell is this whole thing about?

When my eyes found the dead they would go to the face, to see if I could read in their dead expression some hint at what came next, what was felt next, what was experienced next, if anything. Then I'd look at the boots, one almost sure way to identify the dead as one of *ours*. Our Vietnam boots, with their fabric sides and Kevlar inserts, sheathed our feet and made us military. Without them, we looked vulnerable, approachable, touchable.

I was the LT. I heard this exchange. I saw the naked human exposed for what he was, and I wondered if he knew.

All *right* my man . . . I see what you're doin' down there, I see you pullin' at the laces on my boots, tearin' at 'em, rippin' 'em out, yeah, got the left one off . . . now go for the right, uh-huh, I see and I understand . . . *listen* . . . gotta listen to the talk . . .

"What the fuck are you doin', Boner? You look like a god-damned gook rippin' the boots off a dead guy's feet."

"Fuck you, Tolley. I'm just respectin' the dead."

"Respectin' the dead? By pulling Jimmy's boots off his feet while he's layin' there in that poncho waitin' for the chopper to take him and our other KIAs outta here? I mean, what the *fuck*?"

"*Six*. We lost six dead approachin' this sorry-assed piece-of-shit ville, and I'll be goddamned if Jimmy ain't one of 'em."

"What do you mean?"

"Aw, hell. He told me this morning when we got ready to saddle up, said to me, 'Hey, Boner . . . I feel funny this morning, feel like this is gonna be my *last* wake-up.' Shit. I told him to stuff that kind of talk, told him we was just gonna do another day here in the Nam, another walk in the sun, frag some gooks, burn another postcard village, the usual. He shook his head . . . said he had a *feelin'*."

"So why in the hell are you pullin' his boots off?"

. . . Yes, there we go, my man did it, he remembered. . . . There are my feet, *my* feet, the feet of one James you-can-call-me-Jimmy Drake from St. Louis, running back on my high school football team, half owner of a badass Ford Galaxie, heartbreaker of pretty girls, dancer without peer, good soldier, and son of Dixie and James Drake of hometown USA. *My* feet, with me layin' there cold, half-wrapped in that stinkin' green poncho-liner . . . ain't zipped me into no *completely* horrible black plastic body bag yet, 'cause we're still out here in the bush, out here where it *happened*, where we walked toward their little village and they were sittin' there waitin' for us and then there was that roar and that awful sound of someone grunting and screaming and then the sound of wind rushing and now here we are, me and the other five, and there's my man there pullin' my boots off with my two feet layin' there in among the other ten boots. My man understands, he *knows*, and he's doin' it for *me*. Gotta *listen* to the talk . . .

"I'm still waitin' for an answer while we're waitin' for the damned chopper to haul these KIA outta here. You gonna give me an answer about pullin' Jimmy's boots off his feet, Boner? Look how nice and neat you set them beside the trail. Here's our squad waitin' with these dead guys and the rest of the company is already in the fucking ville takin' it *out*. Sarge said we wasted a ton of gooks, man, after we got through that hedgerow, through their first line of fire. He said there was a bunch of dinks in a bunker and they wouldn't come out and the LT kept lookin' back at these dead guys and then they threw a couple of willie-peter grenades into that hole and just *cooked* those people. Said the screams were unfuckingbelievable. Said they shot a bunch tryin' to run out the other side of the ville, found a ton of AK's, SKS rifles, grenades, medical shit, bags of rice and stuff. Good haul. They're torchin' the ville now, fuckin' *burnin'* it, and you sitting here waiting for them to take Jimmy away dead with his whole goddamned chest blown open and you gotta pull his boots off while he's layin' wrapped in that poncho liner. So I ask you again, Boner. *What the fuck?*"

"Listen, Tolley. Jimmy, every time we seen some shit where we lost some guys KIA, you know? He always nudged me when we walked near where the bodies lay. Know how we always collect them into one place so Doc can look at 'em and say for fuckin' sure they're gone *dead*? Jimmy would nudge me to look at them layin' there side by side, fuckin' black brothers, white surfer kinda guys, eye-talians, spics from New York, fat farm boys, fuckin' Arab-lookin' guys, Indians from out west . . . all of 'em. No matter. Jimmy would nudge me and say, 'Check it out, Boner. Look how when they're layin' stretched out together like that no matter who they were or where they were from or whatever the fuck there was that made them who and what they *was*, they got their Army issue Vietnam boots on. All those boots stickin' out of the poncho liners and they all look the same. All the dead guys in their boots.'"

"Okay, so they all looked like dead guys in their boots, Boner. So what?"

"Jimmy told me he didn't want to look like one of them, like some dead guy in a poncho liner with his same-as-everybody-else boots sticking out."

"Well, what the fuck ever happened to wanting to die with your boots *on*?"

"Christ, Tolley. Jimmy *died* with 'em on. Now I've taken them *off*. Look. See his feet shinin' in the morning sunlight? See his feet? Those are *his* feet, only his . . . not some fucking U.S. Army issue green kinda feet in sorry-assed boots layin' there like everybody else, okay? *Okay*, Tolley? You beginning to get the fucking *picture*? Those are *his* feet, goddammit all to hell, Jimmy Drake's feet. Not yours, not mine, not some scum-sucking gook's feet. Understand? *Understand?*"

"Yeah . . . Jesus . . . yeah, Boner, I got it. Take it easy, will ya?"

"Ah, it's okay, Tolley . . . I'm just . . ."

"I know, man."

"Hey, look what else I got."

"No shit, you got Jimmy's Zippo with the map of fucking Vietnam on it."

"Yep. Let's go see if the LT needs any help."

. . . All *right*, my man . . . You did it and I saw you and I . . . oh, man . . . There's that wind, that rushing wind again, and I . . . and I . . .

Illumination

Darkness has depth.

If there is no true black, then there must be green—six greens in shadow layered—giving the darkness of jungle night depth and texture. It could be both comforting and horrifying, that dark, textured tapestry stretched out in front of your position in the night. Sometimes in the highlands it sloped down and away in a clearing that shone almost silver before washing against the fullness of the jungle, the clearing giving the first obvious stretch of depth, followed by the subtle layers in the foliage. Often in the highlands your position was scraped out of the loam *in* the foliage, in the jungle, so the wall of green was *right there*, but still more than one-dimensional. You could reach out your arm, study your pale hand, push it forward into the gloom, and sense . . . distance. In that place, the small hole-in-the-loam place, the wall of jungle seemed to surround you, envelop you, enshroud you.

Because it was night and you were in the jungle in a hole in the loam cradling your M-16 and *they* were out there, you heard . . . things. Your entire absolute being focused through your eyes and ears, augmented by your nose. You opened your mouth slightly to give every possible advantage to those tiny stereo membranes which would not only receive the vibrations from *them*, but would actually help you find the direction those vibrations came from. Your eyes sought any nuance in the six greens that approximated the effect of light, any contrast that might show form, *their* form. You slowly breathed in and out, taking the dank air from the loam and leaves, from the wet and burned. Your senses sorted through the layers of aromas, searching for the acrid smell of sweat, of oil, of nuoc mam sauce and bitter tobacco, for these things signified *them*.

There is, no kidding, that darkness in the jungle so complete you "can't see your hand in front of your face," but even that darkness is not impenetrable. You force your eyes to relax even as the rest of your being lies tight like a tripwire, to relax and watch, *watch* the blackness in front of you, let it turn to green, let it grow into layers and textures, until it becomes a palpable and recognizable still life reaching up toward the canopy and beyond. If that canvas is recognizable, the moment anything within it moves, becomes, or is introduced, *changes anything*, you are instantly aware of its presence. So you tilt your face to the green, relax your eyes, allow your ears to accept the gift of incoming vibrations, open your nostrils to the odors of approaching death, caress the cool and determined steel of your M-16, study the dark canvas before you, and wait.

"Incoming illumination."

Now it all goes silver and black as a strange hiss and whistle waffle down from the sky above the canopy. Silver and black still-life tintype frozen cardboard one-dimensional outlines, layered over and over to create the illusion of depth.

Silver and black, black-black, light-black, crystal silver, dirty silver . . . hiss and whistle. In some odd and disconcerting way the illuminated jungle seems to *leap* at you as it is washed in silver and black. Closer than before, dry, brittle, leaning in on your cold and dirty little hole. Silver and black equals cold . . . it shows on the humid dank stinking hot jungle night and makes it brittle cold, and hard. You won't reach your pale hand out there now, but if you did you are sure it would not be softly enveloped, no. It would hit with a tinny thump, and curl back toward your face with the rigid middle finger extended between your eyes.

Black and silver, black and silver; then . . . it swings, swings up there in its toy parachute, swings and spins and sputters, and the edges of black and silver begin to go sepia, then pale green, flat green, sepia again, silver again, pale green. Now impossible grotesque artificial shadows stretch and pool and form where no shadow was a moment ago. We are illuminated, but blotched in black tufts of shadows like spattered fuzzy ink spots flung across our canvas. The indicators of stage and setting we based our reality on in the dark are now stripped and sullen, stark and brazen, leaping and leaning and reaching for us with edges, edges everywhere that were not there a moment ago. Damn it, whisper your ears, stop that awful hiss and whistle, will you? Crap, huffs your nose, now we get a nice cloud of sulfur and cordite to suck on. Christ, cry your eyes . . . *what the fuck happened to the night?*

Black and silver, stark and angled, straight and hard, and . . . soft. Soft like fabric, smooth like skin. Angled, yes; but more a curve than an angle. Soft, smooth, curved: eggshell. Eggshell, not black and silver, not pale green. Eggshell, and leaning. Leaning out, *breathing* out, breathing *in* and out, trying to be very still. A fuzzy ink spot above the soft smooth curve, featured, with an eye flashing out from the ink. A

searching eye, an eye tripping across the hard black-and-
silver landscape, an eye pulsing with adrenaline and fear, an
eye above widened nostrils, above a dry gaping mouth, above
a carefully lifting and falling chest, an eye above the eggshell
hand on the forestock of his AK-47.

Devil take the night, devil take the black and white, devil
take the green, the silver, the textures, the loam, the dank,
the fear. Devil take the illumination and the darkness. FIRE,
rrriiippp, FIRE, *riiip*, FIRE, FIRE, FIRE. *Boom* claymore.
Boom grenade. *Rip, rip, rip, rip*.

Your eyes see him spin out from the tree trunk, arm flung
toward the ink-spot face, AK slamming off two green tracers
into the canopy. No tracers from you, just *rip, rip, rip*. Your
eyes see the black and his spastic twisting death. Your ears
embrace his screams, your nose hungrily savors the aroma of
cooking M-16, your mouth digs around for enough saliva to
spit out the words, *DIE MOTHERFUCKER DIE DIE DIE
YOU FUCKING MOTHERFUCKER DIE DIE DIE.*

It stops.

You sob, then take a deep ragged breath.

Somewhere nearby a low moan won't end, somewhere
nearby someone calls for his mother in a language you don't
speak.

Darkness has depth.

Face of War

IT was a hot and clear day on Highway 14 between Pleiku and Kontum, and I was with an ARVN armored
unit on convoy security duty. Dak To, to our north, had been
getting hit hard, and the large truck convoys ran almost every
morning on resupply runs. The highway was in pretty good
shape through our area, paved, with ditches along the shoulders, and cleared fire zones almost fifty meters from the road
to the edge of the tangled and ever-encroaching jungle. This
gave our firepower an advantage because even if the NVA
used a crew-served weapon, B-40 rockets, or mortars on a
convoy—attempting to disable the lead and trail vehicles—
the moment they charged out of the undergrowth to run
toward the trucks we could take them under fire. The major
disadvantages for us included the natural fact that the roadway snaked between hills and low mountains, which gave the
NVA the high ground to work from, and the bureaucratic fact
that the loaded convoys always headed north at the same time
in the mornings. Usually the roadway was swept by engineers

for mines before the first trucks came through, and the ARVN unit I was with positioned their T-41 tanks and M113 APC's at all the *most likely spots* for ambush.

On this day I sat in a jeep with my Recon and RTO, catching some rays, waving at the occasional trucker as he rumbled past, wondering who John Galt really was, and monitoring the radio nets for any sounds of action. The ARVN armored unit was a pretty good one, with a commander who kept the men trained and the equipment in good running order, and who would not shy away from a fight if one began. If something *did* start I already had artillery, helicopter gunships, and Air Force fast-movers aware of my preselected targets. My Recon and RTO were in the middle of a heated discussion about the relative taste quality of a char-broiled hamburger eaten at a beach joint in southern California and the same burger consumed in a neighborhood bar in Manhattan: "Yes, Lieutenant, I *do* mean in *New*-the-absolutely-only-real-city-in-the-entire-world-*York*."

Almost without turning my head I had a clear view of an ARVN armored personnel carrier squatting a few feet away from the tree line. For a moment I had the surrealistic impression that it was a steel box taking a quick deep breath, like an immediate and intense expansion. Then the vehicle commander, who had been standing in the cupola behind a .50-caliber machine gun, exited the hatch straight up into the clear sky. He kept his legs close together, the toes of his boots pointed downward. His arms waved gracefully as he ascended, his head thrown back, still covered by his helmet. A thin column of blue-gray smoke followed his boots, and he began to spin slowly as he reached the apogee of his flight. As he slowed to a stop, tilted, then flipped over and headed face-first toward his APC there came a muted *whompf,* and a gush of dirty orange flame filled the interior of the vehicle.

I've always wondered if he was still alive as he rocketed above us all, if he looked peacefully down upon us, upon the NVA soldier who had fired the rocket-propelled grenade into the side of his APC, upon all the other NVA soldiers who were even then firing their AK's and charging out of the tree line. I shit you not, he flew fifty, sixty feet straight up as the APC exploded, and he would have had a primo view of the first few seconds of the battle.

Even as we observed the APC commander's flight, the feral part of our brains told us what had occurred, and we tumbled out of the jeep into the ditch clutching M-16's and radio handsets. The bulk of the convoy was already to our north, but the NVA leader must have felt it was worth it to spring the ambush on the last dozen or so trucks lumbering past our position. The raw earth around the cooking tracked vehicle suddenly swarmed with NVA soldiers in two-tone green, rubber sandals, pith helmets, and backpacks, armed with AK's, B-40's, and satchel charges, firing and yelling as they came. In those first chaotic seconds I actually gave thought to pulling the rest of the APC crew out of their flaming box, but the fire baked off the tracks' fuel and ammo, and through the open rear ramp I clearly saw three blackened dwarf figures curled into fetal twists, FUBAR.

Armored troops get to "button up." When the APC exploded and the ambush was sprung, all tank and APC crews simply dropped into their vehicles, slammed the hatches home, and jammed their mounts into gear. They immediately moved to escape any *more* rockets, and began to swing their guns around for targets. Fine. Their raggedy-ass attached red-leg FO, however, could not button up . . . unless you count the pucker factor. Recon, RTO, and I could only hunker down in the ditch beside our jeep, radio for artillery fire into the tree line, and try not to get in the way of all the hot flying metal. The word "eruption" works when applied to the roar of weapon noise that enveloped us, taking the peaceful morning and tearing it asunder, taking the spit out of our mouths, the breath out of our lungs, and most rational thought out of our minds.

Machine-gun fire came from the tree line, along with the occasional roar-*whoosh* of a rocket. The *crump* of mortars or grenades punctuated the steady staccato punch of AK's and M-16's; here and there all of this was punctuated with a thin scream or hoarse yell. Within seconds the artillery I had called for pounded into the tree line all along the area the NVA had first come from, and this only added to the storm. At the very height of the barrage, I felt a tug on my sleeve, turned to look into the sweating face of my Recon, and heard him say in a calm voice, "We wasted two crawling up to your jeep on this side, LT, but these goddamned ARVN tanks roaring around all over the place are scaring the piss outta me." I nodded, looked at my inert M-16 lying nearby, and went back to the radio. I had a team of gunships standing by, and wanted to have the ARTY hold while they made a couple of runs.

The change as a battle peaks is very subtle, but an experienced ear can discern it. Slowly, fitfully, the fire began to ease off; the yelling, the booming began to ebb. We cautiously lifted our heads and after a moment saw the first tank commanders open their hatches and look around. We saw one other APC burning near the trees, and one truck belly-flopped in the middle of the roadway on its frame. The rest of it, wheels, cargo bed, cab, engine, was scattered all around, blackened and twisted. "That explains that unfuckingbelievable explosion right in the middle of this shit-assed ambush, huh, LT?" RTO gazed at the remains of what had probably been an ammo truck. I said nothing. I had not heard the explosion. We spent a few more minutes working the ARTY and gunships on likely routes the enemy might take as they didi'd to their regroup points, then closed down the radio nets and went for a stroll to see how it all came out.

Most of the NVA lying in their impossible postures of sprawling death were young and fit, their uniforms in good repair, fresh haircuts as always. Their bodies were mangled by the fire they'd taken as they charged and died. Many had missing limbs, torn chest and stomach cavities, wet mucusy blossoming exploded skulls, soupy brains, ropey entrails, clutching hands, and the always interesting perfect-left-foot-still-sandal-shod. The ferocity of our combined fires left no prisoners. If they remained on the field, they were most assuredly dead.

We had dead, too. The crew of both APC's had died, every last man, including the human cannonball whose launch had kicked things off and the American who had been driving the ammo. We found him on the side of the road about a hundred feet from the skeletal remains of his truck. He appeared to be sitting in a tight spider hole dug into the shoulder next to the ditch; we could see nothing below the bottom edge of his flak jacket. He sat there like that—intact in his flak jacket, still wearing his helmet, his muscular arms sleeveless but unblemished where they came out of the jacket, his hands still grasping the steering wheel of his truck, his pale face with its rust-colored bushy mustache and bulging eyes staring north after his comrades who had gone on without him. The thick pool of blood that had seeped out of him darkened the earth. We walked away from him in silence. I heard later an MP was beaten senseless by some truckers when he tried to take a photo.

It is nearly impossible to describe or evoke the incredible firestorm created by modern weapons of war, and their effect on the human body. You have heard the stories, perhaps seen photos. When explosive steel impacts human flesh the effects often strain visual credulity. Your mind looks twice. There is no posture of death on the battlefield too outlandish, too impossible, too macabre. I have walked in the sad and distorted landscape of the dead, and have stared at unrecognizable parts of men, and dead men whose apparently unblemished bodies looked serene in repose. The hideous randomness and impartiality of it offered me no rest.

Near our jeep we found the Face of the Enemy. It was the face of an NVA soldier, cleanly cut as if with a scalpel, the line straight across his skull above his eyebrows, then down in front of his ears, curving along his jaw and chin, then back around. Everything behind the face had been scooped away. There was no decapitated body nearby, simply the face, eyes open and staring, lying slightly curved in the dirt. It had the look of a wax mask, synthetic somehow, the skin smooth and unblemished. The mouth was curved into a frown, and I studied it a moment before turning away to vomit. When finished I wiped my mouth on my sleeve, pointed at the face in the dirt, and said to Recon and RTO in a shaky voice, "All we need is a couple of pieces of ribbon and another one like that, except laughing. . . . "

They both stared at me blankly, and never asked me to explain.

Topographical Error

WE had beaucoup heavy machinery on the ground, diesel-powered terrain modifiers, grunting and roaring, making the ground into a place *we* wanted to fight. Need to throw a bridge over that river? Not a problem. Bothersome hill making a mockery of a planned roadbed? Step aside, son. Ground too wet for an airstrip? Go have lunch, bring back a jet. Mountain in the way of the view? Here, hold my hat.

I heard we Americans were not true jungle fighters because we ripped out the jungle, flattened hills and ridges, and created perfectly clear fire zones. Sounds like sour grapes to me. Poor Uncle Ho. He read what Sun Tzu said about choosing to fight only where your strength meets the enemy's weakness. Another example of what sounds good over a cup of tea getting bulldozed by the realities of war.

In our efforts to take the war to them, we did fight them on their terms, too. We moved quietly from the sunlight into the green, into the gloom, into the moist and treacherous jungle-world arena to seek out and destroy the wily Viet. He lived and worked there, in the gloom. Of course he did. If he stuck his head out of the bushes to see what he could see he got a quick look at paved roads, lots of trucks, tanks, helicopters, airstrips, bunkers, mess halls, movie theaters, huge PX's, Bob Hope and his girls, and pissed-off guys with all the toys of war. He was usually killed by those pissed-off guys, so he stayed in the green gloom. When a fight *did* occur deep in the bowels of Indian country, right where the wily Viet wanted to fight his wily fight, where he was set up and *prepared* to do battle with the clumsy and burdened U.S. troops (even the cumbersome straight-leg infantry units heavy with gear and fragrant with aftershave and smoke) more often than not the wily Viet would find himself dead.

It has been almost gleefully argued that when the North Viets finally *did* (I wasn't there then, were you?) come roaring down on the hapless and totally fucked South, they did it on those wonderful roads and across those amazing bridges built by all that heavy American equipment and know-how. True. And now those same roads and bridges carry to the grasping and gasping North all those grunting and chuffing Coca-cola, Nike, Mickey D's, Gear, World Bank, American Express, Hilton, and Levi's trucks.

Now the wily Viet is hungry, so he tries to sell us the remains of our missing dead in exchange for something he can suck on.

Spitter

INTELLIGENT, determined, brave, driven by idealism, pneumatically nubile.

Hungry recipient of ejaculated dogma, but a spitter . . . not a swallower.

Lied to by smiling freedom fighters, encouraged to embrace the photogenic amputees while leaning on the crutches of altruism.

Confidently attempted to stop the flow of blood by driving a stake through our heart. Attempted to perform CPR by blowing smoke up our ass.

Starred in the pornographic snuff-film *Clueless in Hanoi*. Poor Jane.

Silk in the Wire

SHE was a flawless example of the Southeast Asian child. The daughter of an ARVN soldier and his camp-follower wife, she was six or seven years old. She had perfect straight black hair, worn long and cut in bangs, a slim and healthy body, a cream-to-caramel complexion, and big dark eyes. She wore cheap rubber shower sandals, black shorts, and a white long-sleeve top. Like most Viet children when around Americans, she watched everything, followed everything with her eyes.

This time my little three-man unit was attached to an ARVN lookout post for a couple of days, to assist in calling artillery or airstrikes if the OP came under attack. There had been a few small probes and one light mortar attack on the OP in the last week, so there was a chance it was on the hit list. For an ARVN setup it wasn't in bad shape, good fighting holes all tied in nicely around the perimeter, strong bunkers in good repair, the soldiers carrying well-maintained weapons

and appearing alert, and plenty of wire between the perimeter and the tree line a couple of hundred feet away.

She went out into the wire.

It was the middle of a bright and breezy morning. The OP
had a campground feel to it; the smell of cooking fires, gear
being checked or repaired, children playing here and there.
The night had gone, a quiet, watchful night punctuated by
the burst of sporadic illumination flares, and the dawn had
rolled in with no enemy in sight. Once the sun was up strong
the campers came out of their holes, my team included, and
prepared to spend a relaxed day.

The wire was strung in five or six rows outward from the
first fighting holes. It was the standard barbed wire, curled
here and there around a mounting stake, the new stuff twisted with the old. It seemed like there was always old stuff
around those OP's. Good high ground is always good high
ground, no matter what war is being fought over the ground
at the time. The French had once occupied this area, and they
supposedly placed some of the fragmented and rusted wire
around us. A lot of stuff lay around out in the wire: old shell
casings, ration boxes, the occasional silk parachute from a
flare or supply drop.

Maybe that's what she went out there for, the silk. It was
pretty, and the family could sell it on the black market. We sat
around our gear watching as she poked and picked through
the different rows of wire. No one else took notice. All the
ARVN's, men and women, seemed to be busy adjusting to
their lazy morning, hanging in hammocks, squatting and
smoking, weaving hats from long blades of grass, wiping the
last dregs of rice from their pots. The little girl belonged to
them, but she was in the wire.

She felt our American eyes on her once. She stood, turned

a half-circle, smiled, and waved a small child's wave. We waved back, three grown American soldiers grinning stupidly and waving for all we were worth. She hesitated, then went back to her explorations. After a moment we saw movement in the wire, and so did she. We could not make out her words, but the tone was severe as she admonished the one who followed her stealthily. Must have been the pain-in-the-butt little brother, four years old, maybe less. He wore ragged black shorts, no shirt, no shoes. His tummy bulged and his black hair stood straight up in spiky tufts. If he heard his sister's words ordering him back to their bunker he gave no sign, but plodded toward her resolutely now that he had been discovered.

My Recon, checking over the PRC-25 radio sitting on the ground between his legs, turned his head, spit, and said to me, "I don't think they should let their damn kids play out in that wire—" The rest of his opinion was lost in the roar of the explosion. The area where the children had stood instantly became a hammering, pulsing, buffeting cloud, angry red-orange and greasy black-gray. Dirt and debris flew up and out as the roar washed over us and the OP. Just as quickly it was gone, blown away by the breeze, the wire still stretched around the perimeter, the forever jungle two hundred feet away a silent witness to the act.

The ARVN all jumped up and ran to the edge of the wire, looking toward where the girl lay. My Recon shouldered between them, the wails from the women already stretching toward crescendo, and walked through. I hesitated, then followed, trying not to seek out his bootprints in the dust, trying to let my boots find their *own* safe ground. He got to them first. No, not them . . . her. The little boy was simply no longer there. The girl was conscious. Her big eyes were wide open, and as Recon knelt beside her those eyes went to his face, and she smiled and shrugged. Then she took one flut-tering last breath and was still. She was gone from her perfect curl of a belly button on down, no legs, no hips, no bottom, no nothing. No big flood of blood, either, just pale skin end-ing in flaps, like hastily cut fringe. Recon scooped her up in his big sunburned hands, turned, and carried her to the wail-ing women and silent men. His face was a mask, but very red, and as he brushed past me I could see the blood on his bottom lip where his teeth had dug in.

Most of the ARVN's were talking loudly in their own lan-guage, but a few, including the scout assigned as our contact with the unit, had English. These let fly in words they knew we'd understand.

"It was a mine, a big one."

"*We* didn't put out any big mines, only little ones. *We* only put out trip flares and claymores. *We* didn't make this kinda booby trap in wire . . ."

"French. It was some old French bomb they left buried there. Goddamned French left their shit in our wire."

"I bet it is You-Ess. I bet it some kinda You-Ess stuff . . . maybe other Americans here before, maybe *they* left it, or maybe VC find You-Ess stuff Americans allatime leave laying around and make it into booby trap for us."

"*We* didn't leave *that* kinda mine out there."

It became harder to hear them as the women took off. They squatted beside the incomplete girl Recon had laid gen-tly on a poncho on the ground, their bony hands clasped in front of their flat breasts, their brownish-red gaping mouths stretched into lopsided oblongs as they bent their heads back, stretched the cords in their necks, and fucking *wailed*.

Recon took it as long as he could. Then, his face red and mottled, he stood with his hands clenched into fists at his sides, put *his* head back, and roared, "God-*damn*-it!" The

Viets all froze, staring at him wide-eyed. After a moment he seemed to realize what effect he had had, looked at the up-turned faces sadly, and said, "Oh . . . I'm sorry." Then he turned and walked out of their circle and away from the little half-girl. The Viets seemed to respect his reaction, waited for him to clear their group, then took up their shrieking and wailing again.

My RTO sat with our gear. He had not lifted his head after his first glimpse after the explosion, willing the act invalid if his eyes did not record it. Recon strode past him to the other side of the perimeter where he stood and gazed out toward the jungle, his back straight.

I took one last look at the girl as I backed away. Her eyes had closed, her face beautiful in sleep. Clenched in the fist of her right hand was a short length of tattered silk. Her other hand was open, but empty.

Patriot

ERNARD Fall wrote about the Mang Yang Pass on Highway 19 west of An Khe. He chronicled how one of the French Mobile Armored Groups drove into a nice Viet Minh ambush there and was destroyed. Bernard couldn't stop himself from predicting that the same terrible thing would happen to the Americans when *they* tried to fight the Viets. The Viet had this indomitable will and spirit. The Viet was strong and brave and resourceful. The Viet was tricky and vicious, and most of all, the Viet was a patriot soldier who could not be defeated by big armies with big equipment, big mouths, and big egos. Big armies brought lots of fat targets for the Viets to shoot at, making sure the cameras were rolling as female Viets—always smiling with patriotic fervor and dutiful determination as they made war—machine-gunned sweating French soldiers.

The Viet could march through impassable jungle thick with heat and insects without getting lost, existing on the water he licked from leaves and one ball of rice a day. The Viet could carry three weapons and enough ammo for a platoon, all the while singing the patriotic songs of his lovely and besieged homeland. The Viet could slip through any perimeter security, could slither through barbed wire, loaded with explosives and the will to die for Uncle Ho, and could live without harm under a torrent of impotent bombs from B-52's. Basically, according to the French war journalist desperate to explain the low count of real testicles in the French army command, the Viet was simply the most beautiful, motivated, powerful, effective soldier the world had ever seen.

We came upon a group of these same described Viet soldiers early one misty morning. They were taking a shit, very much like any common human being. Outstanding jungle fighters that they were, they had neglected to post security while they went about this business, so while they shit we gunned them down and they flipped and flopped and spun and died. *Shittus interruptus.* My goodness . . . *we* were certainly impressed with how very *Viet* the Viets were.

Real Estate

I'VE already mentioned the American landscape we built over what was Vietnam—that is, the roads, airfields, ports, movie theaters, PX's, division-headquarters cities with their own police and fire departments, and the EM, NCO, and Officers Clubs. Don't forget those nice hootches for the generals, either; air-conditioning, swimming pools, the occasional tennis court. Supposedly there was a Vietnam under all of that, but who knew? Before us it was the French; the Japanese were there for a while, the Chinese too. Maybe it's a *rumor* that there ever was a Vietnam; in reality it was simply a place where other cultures pitched their tents.

Where I'm going with this is that old song about the VC and NVA soldiers "owning" pieces of terrain or sections of the twenty-four-hour clock. "Charlie owns the night," the somber journalist would say as he crouched for the carefully sighted camera near a damaged U.S. tank beside the road. "Charlie owns the jungle. . . . Charlie owns the mountains. . . . Charlie owns the delta, the villages, the rice paddies, the

trails, the rivers, the hearts and minds of the people."
Carefully chosen words and video footage would seem to validate this observation, as given to us by that learned and
"combat-hardened" journalist, and for years people sucked it
down.

Let me give you a little hint here. Is it perception, or per-
version? Why don't we begin with that always popular "Charlie owns the night"? Yes, he did spend a lot of time moving
around on the trails and waterways at night. He moved men
and matériel, removed wounded, brought in propaganda,
revenue collectors, and political cadres. He prepared rocket,
mortar, and jump-off positions, marched into peaceful sleep-
ing villages to extort rice and hiding places, and to put into effect a draft that made ours look enlightened. (They didn't get
a letter in the mail, they got a gun to the head.) He crept
stealthily through the jungle following little markers of wet
bark and leaves, to form up outside the wire of our com-
pounds in readiness for attack. He did all those things related
to political, terrorist, and military movement in the dark . . .
at night. Is it necessary to discuss here what would have happened to those movements had they been made in *daylight*?

Yeah, well. We know if he stuck his head out in the daylight on any of his missions he usually wound up extremely
dead in a very short time. I would argue *we* owned the daylight. What happened when we decided to go out into his
jungle during his night? Many are the times, all over Vietnam, the highlands, the coast, the North, the delta, when
Mister Charles was going about his nocturnal business when
the very *world* suddenly became a roaring hellish place of
tearing steel and tumbling explosions, and Charles may or
may *not* have had time to scream as he died in a hail of shot.
American soldiers were out there too, out in that spooky
nighttime jungle, out in *Charlie's* night. Even though most of

them had only been soldiers for a little over a year, in combat a couple of months, as opposed to the accolade-garnering Viet soldier who was a soldier for life and had been fighting righteous wars while we were still gumming nipples (are we not often reminded of those proud Viets who waged war against the soft Americans even as they had made war against the effete French?), somehow the American kids found their way to a position in the dark and waited for Charles to arrive *so they could kill him.*

What about when Charlie crept up to the edge of our wire and waited for the whistle-signal to attack us in the night? Yes—as our hard-jowled journalist was quick to show us—occasionally the VC or NVA had their act together, the timing was right, the weather bad enough to hinder air support, and they actually overran a position. Might be a Popular Forces outpost, a Special Forces camp, an artillery firebase or a company-sized LP, or maybe even the city of Hue or a part of Saigon. Sure enough, the NVA would blast the wire, mortar or RPG the gun positions, machine-gun the towers, and come swarming in, firing from the hip as they came. Sure enough, the defense would collapse, Americans would die or be captured, the wounded would hide and pray for the dawn. Sure enough, the NVA would mill around for a while ransacking and rummaging, torturing the dying, until the first streaks of morning light. Then they would quickly fade back into the jungle, dragging their dead by the length of line their soldiers tied to their own ankles before battle for just that purpose. Like a vampire eager to escape the sunlight, Charles had to scamper into the darkness of the jungle; like any good bloodsucker, if a VC stayed around too long he burned.

Mostly, when Charles came shrilling and shooting up into the perimeter wire he died there. We met him with all the tools of war; behind the tools were frightened, angry, and determined men. When they came at the wire in bunches they died in bunches. When they crawled into the wire in pairs they died in pairs. When they managed to wiggle through and charge the bunkers in single-handed desperation they died alone, their bodies literally shot to pieces.

Is this a good place to stop and discuss their quality of leadership? Their tactics? What about the vaunted and revered General Giap? Giap is considered by so many to be the greatest military genius of modern times, brilliant, incomparable. What a bunch of bullshit. Want to argue about military war versus political war? Immediate combat goals versus long-range political goals? (Careful, now . . . how long-range would you like to go?) Fine. Talk to me later. Politics is a whore to war, and war is an abusive husband to politics. I'm talking about a military leader in charge of managing and directing his soldiers. General Giap, student of Sun Tzu, follower of Uncle Ho, admirer of man's history of war, victor over the French, sent his soldiers out time after time to charge into our firepower and die. They were at their best in ambush and booby trap, at their worst in frontal assault. But still he sent them. The whistles would blow, the mortars would begin to fall, and General Giap's misled faithful would leap to their feet and charge. And die.

What about Khe Sanh? Yep, the Marines had a tough time up there, and yeah, as a part of that Special Forces camp at Lang Vei was overrun by the NVA using Russian tanks for the first time. Michael Herr's famous airstrip at Khe Sanh—the one with all the "bones of aircraft" photogenically scattered around—was a place where only *four* major aircraft were lost during the entire campaign. After they were *told to* the Marines left, carrying out their dead and wounded. Got another little hint for you here. If the Marines had been told to stay *they would still be there*. Poor LBJ had the ghost of "Din

Bin Phoo" tickling his prostate, but the French were defeated and overrun at Dien Bien Phu, while the Marines dug in and defended an indefensible position until ordered to leave. Gee, am I not giving the brilliant Giap credit for keeping Westmoreland's bushy eyebrows pointed north while the wily Viets moved into their attacking positions for the grand Tet Offensive? Okay, I bow to Giap for letting all those Viet soldiers die around Khe Sanh so their compatriots could prepare to die everywhere else during Tet.

What about Tet? Hue, Saigon? Okay. What about them? General Giap managed to scare the piss out of a bunch of American journalists, who then tailored their reports home to scare the piss out of already doubtful moms and their hound-dog president. In reality it was the same old General Giap brilliance in action. Yeah, the NVA occupied the sacred city of Hue for weeks. They executed thousands of their own intellectual, artistic, and freedom-seeking brothers—Now where is your camera, journalist? Now where is that erect microphone? Now where is your stormy brow while you ask the NVA and their brilliant leader the *really tough questions?*— and they left piles of trash and feces everywhere. Again, the Marines took heavy losses. Boys were maimed and died, buildings were lost to the NVA, whole parts of the city, even the Citadel. But again, predictably, the NVA died. Did the VC and NVA ever "own" anything, or did they just borrow it for a few minutes, like one of those pay toilets in France?

Don't forget—certainly our wizened and condescending journalist won't let you forget this—the *American Embassy*, right in downtown Saigon. Why, the brilliantly led, indomitable, wily, gallant NVA infiltrators actually blasted their way into the embassy courtyard (excuse me, unbiased journalist, did you say *courtyard* or *compound*?). They ran around firing their weapons and *raised their flag*. Was it four of them, or seven? Were they there twenty minutes, three hours, or two days? Did they live or die?

In case you have not been paying attention, *they died.*

Almost before the all-knowing and courageous journalist filed his crippling story about how the American Embassy had *fallen*, the place was open for business as usual. The broken glass, torn flag, scattered papers, bodies, and feces (why did they always *shit* everywhere?) were swept away. The politicians, bureaucrats, military staff, doughnut dollies, CIA spooks, and secretaries went back to their desks . . . and the poor misrepresented flag went right back up the pole.

Even if the revered General Giap had his nuoc mam sauce delivered in fifty-five-gallon drums, it still would not be enough to mask the stench of rotting NVA and VC bodies putrefying over the soil of his places of victory.

Enough. In the war most of us saw, every time the NVA or VC came out to fight we killed them. When they came at night we killed them. When they came in the daylight, we killed them. When they ambushed us in the highlands, attacked our outposts in the delta or our perimeter up by the DMZ, we killed them.

Did they wound and maim us? Sometimes.

Did they kill us? Sometimes.

Did they die? Almost every time we met.

Friendly Fire

In the midst of carnage and fear there would come moments when the hard and certain realities of war would be suspended long enough for us to look at ourselves and perhaps laugh. It was a rough humor, to be sure, black comedy at its darkest, but it was genuine, and it reflected imperfections and inadequacies in us we held dear.

We were bringing up the rear of a long truck convoy headed north on Highway 14, out of Pleiku headed for the besieged Dak To. It was the morning run, and it was ambushed. The lead trucks were hit with B-40 rocket fire, mortars fell all along the line, and machine-gun and AK fire raked the trucks as the drivers tried to keep moving and not get forced off the road. The NVA unit that sprang the ambush even sent a few squads of sappers and riflemen tumbling out of the jungle to charge the trucks—they were firing, screaming, and hoping to blow up some Americans with their explosive packs. To do this they had to run several hundred feet across cleared flat ground, in the open and exposed. Most died long before they reached the trucks.

Seconds after the ambush began I was yelling on several radio channels calling for artillery on prearranged targets along the tree line, and getting air support on standby in case things really got ugly. Since my RTO and I were in our thin-skinned jeep, and since within a few seconds the roar of the ambush and answering fires reached a deafening pitch, we opted to slew the jeep into a ditch, bail out, run a few feet, and dive into a shallow fighting hole to better conduct our business. The hole had three or four old sandbags lined up as a firing parapet, facing the jungle. We saw no enemy soldiers, but small arms and mortar fire was hitting on the road behind us and up and down the ranks of ARVN armored units assigned to protect the convoy.

Once or twice I half-straightened from my crouch in the hole, pointed the barrel of my M-16 toward the tree line, and fired off a few bursts. Then I returned to my ARTY coordination on the radio, but yelled at my RTO to continue the fire toward the enemy with his M-79 grenade launcher, which we lovingly called the bloop gun. This weapon looked like a pregnant sawed-off shotgun with an angular wooden stock. It was breech-loaded with a fat bulbous round—sort of looked like the old .22 bullet on steroids—which was really a 40mm grenade. The weapon had good range and accuracy, and to help protect the man firing the weapon the round was not armed until it had made thirteen revolutions after leaving the barrel. If you accidentally shot it into the dirt at your feet, it would not explode.

I was busy on the radios, but did have time to observe that my RTO was not enthusiastic about raising his body or head to fire the M-79 at the enemy. Possibly he thought the hole we occupied was too shallow, perhaps he thought if the enemy reacted to our fire and discovered our radios he would make a special effort to blast us, maybe he didn't *care* who controlled Highway 14, II Corps, Vietnam, *or* Capitol Hill. Be that as it may, when I heard the satisfying "thunk" sound of the bloop gun I glanced up and saw he was firing toward the tree line without really taking aim. He remained in his low crouch, one shoulder toward the enemy, and would rise slightly with his head and face down to point the barrel out of our hole and fire the round. I went back to work, quietly acknowledging that most soldiers in combat simply fire their weapons toward where they think the enemy is; they rarely point at an individual target. Many soldiers in the heat of combat will not fire their weapons at all. At least my RTO was shooting.

Then came an odd thing. Over the radio nets I clearly heard indications that the fight was ending. Fire missions were being canceled, word was passed that we would need no helicopter gunships or other air support, ARTY batteries were shutting down. Off in the distance to my right, I saw the last of the trucks continuing north, and here and there soldiers from the ARVN unit were opening the hatches of their tanks. All of this was odd because to *our* immediate front the ambush was still in full swing. True, no machine-gun fire could be heard, but there was a steady rain of incoming mortar fire. The *crump, crruummp, crrruuummmp* of their rounds continued to blast clods of dirt into the air around us, accompanied by a sprinkling of hot shrapnel. Had we been specifically targeted because of those damning radio antennas? Was there a squad of suicidal NVA soldiers determined to fight us to the death even though their compatriots had already died or fled? I wondered as I crouched lower in the hole, heartened by the bold tenacity of my RTO, who—like a deadly metronome— kept loading and shooting, loading and shooting.

Finally one of the American advisers to the ARVN radioed and asked, "What's going on down there with you, two-niner?" I compared the rhythm of my RTO's firing with the incoming explosions of the enemy mortar fire. They matched perfectly.

Sensing it was okay to do so, I leaned back to take a closer look at my man in action. Sure enough, each time he loaded his M-79 he pointed the barrel toward the tree line and squeezed the trigger. Problem was, he had hunkered lower and lower in the hole, a prudent move not unknown to most veterans, and each time he fired the weapon the round exited the barrel, caromed off the old sandbags, and shot almost straight up into the air. This gave the round plenty of time to arm itself as it spun toward its highest point, so when it tipped at the end of its flight and headed for the ground after having described a *very* narrow arc, it was ready to blow. As my RTO was determined to put out as much fire against his enemy as possible, he had at least two rounds in the air at once, occasionally *three*. And these well-intentioned rounds then came down to explode *right in front of our sorry little hole scraped out of the raggedy-ass dirt somewhere on the west side of a lonely road to nowhere.*

We were mortaring ourselves.

After banging on my RTO's shoulder long enough to make him *stop* for a moment, and after explaining that the battle was *over,* and after describing for him why *we* thought *we* were still *in* battle, I sat back, crossed my arms over my commissioned officer's chest, and waited for his response.

RTO hugged the hot barrel of his bloop gun, stroked the unlovely stock, looked at all the smoking shell holes around our position, stuck out his jaw, and said with conviction, "Defensive fire, LT. I was puttin' out a wall of steel, *protectin'* us from an infantry attack on our position. It was my wall-of-steel defensive fire, LT." Then he just looked at me.

Such a plausible explanation. Had either of us been hit by a piece of our defensive fire, I would have put us in for the Purple Heart *and* the Bronze Star.

Longest Night

HE was one of the guys sent down to the sluggish stream at the base of the hill on a water detail, to fill up as many canteens as they could carry and return to the company-sized overnight position. They were a loose-and-tumble squad as they went down, not worried about noise discipline; the company itself had been humping and hacking its way through the area all day. There had been no sightings of enemy soldiers, no contacts for several days. It had been the same old sweat-your-ass-off-while-you-hump-the-bush. They had just reached the bottom on the upslope side of the stream when they took a searing burst of AK fire through the squad at hip level. Probably a small VC or NVA hit team waiting at the stream for just such an opportunity. There was that one burst—our guys all dove and ate dirt for a moment—then nothing more.

Except the screams.

All of the full-metal-jacketed rounds from the AK ripped through air, leaves, and a few pieces of web equipment, except one. One hot heavy chunk of lead blasted from the barrel of the AK, crossed the stream, and penetrated the lower stomach of a young blond guy who had been standing there unscrewing the cap off a canteen. The bullet punched through the thin fabric of his jungle utilities and ate right through all the layers of skin on his belly; then, like a rampaging ferocious hornet-piranha, it chewed into his guts. He was knocked back off his feet and fell on his ass kicking and screaming, dropping the canteen and reaching with splayed fingers for his bursting belly. His companions fired a few ragged bursts into the foliage on the other side of the stream, grabbed him as he writhed and bucked, and dragged him up the winding trail back to the company position.

The position was in hill-to-mountain, double-to-triple canopy terrain in the Central Highlands. The company had about seventy men, light weapons, and one medic. They had already settled into their night position when the water squad was sent down. Their position had been radioed in, as well as their preplanned fires in case they were hit. Theirs was more of a recon-in-force than a search-and-destroy mission, and as an Artillery Forward Observer I had been with them only a couple of mostly uneventful days. The night before we had been subjected to a light rain of 60mm mortar fire, which hopscotched around and through the position blowing clods of dirt, dust, and smoke into the air, but no one had been hurt. It was shrugged off by the veteran grunts and gave the new troops a little trial-by-fire they could feel good about while they waited for their boots to get scuffed and their fatigues to get that nice *worn* look.

But on this night, as the sky grew dark and the surrounding jungle grew darker, the screaming boy with the belly wound was dragged into our perimeter. The company commander, a gawky red-haired lieutenant; the company sergeant, an older stocky E-6 with a shaved head; and the skinny, pimply-faced medic all hustled over to where they dragged the guy in and dumped him into a shallow fighting hole.

The sergeant took one look at the entrails bubbling out from between the screaming kid's fingers, spit, and said, "Shit."

The gawky lieutenant looked down at the kid, then out past the perimeter of foxholes into the darkness that cloaked the jungle, and said, "Give him something, Doc, give him something. Make him stop screaming like that."

The medic went to work. He pried the kid's hands away from the wound. He pulled off the kid's equipment web gear and opened his trousers. He ripped open the jungle-fatigue shirt and used a wipe to clean the area around the seeping and pulsing hole. At the same time he wiped the kid's brow, leaned over his face, and tried to calm him. "Hey . . . hey . . . It's okay, it's all right. Hang on, buddy, hang on now. You're gonna be okay, gonna go home, your ass is gonna be in some clean hospital bed with a couple of sweet nurses to make you feel better. . . . C'mon, man, you gotta be tough now, be strong. . . . "

The kid just screamed.

The medic got out a four-inch compress and taped it neatly in place. He used his other hand to explore the kid's back and bottom to confirm there was no exit wound. He got out a morphine pack and stuck it into the kid's thigh. He talked to him the whole time, but the kid continued to scream.

The sergeant and lieutenant had a conversation.

"We've got to medevac this dude, LT, right now."

"RTO has already been on the net, Sarge. No way they'll send a nighttime evac because of the terrain, the weather, and the enemy activity—"

"Enemy activity has been *shit*, LT, this is the goddamned highlands and the chopper pilots fly up here all the time, and the fucking weather ain't no better or worse than it ever is here in the wonderful tropics."

"I told 'em it was a critical WIA, Sarge. They said no can do, and hold out till daybreak for the first chopper up."

"Bullshit. This is bullshit."

The lieutenant looked down at the medic kneeling beside the wounded boy, and asked, "Doc—can't you hit him with some more sauce to put him *out*? We can't have this scream-ing. It will pinpoint our pos to every gook in the area."

The medic looked through his black plastic Army-issue glasses and responded evenly, "Can give him what I can give him, sir, no more. Fucker's gotta be bleeding inside all *over* the place. I can stick this compress on the shit sticking out of his belly, but I can't do a *damn* thing about the internal dam-age. I can only give him so much juice, and only so often—"

The kid screamed.

Each of us who did the time with the kid on that muggy-hot and cloudy Central Highlands night in the jungle sweat and green darkness probably has his own name for it, or way of giving it a special place in the rucksack of steaming and poisonous memories we carry. To me it has always been sim-ply "The Night of the Belly Wound." It became a concert of sorts, a demonstration, a forum on life, a monologue on pain and fear, a song of death sung by a war protester. I was privi-leged to attend, and even on that night I—through senses begging for release—I understood his eloquence. I had a real bad seat as recipient of his pontifications, but his entire audi-ence had bad seats. We were there.

There are screams of fright and screams of delight, orgas-mic screams, angry screams, fake screams, and the screams of the bereaved. This guy's screams were a symphony, a filibuster, an eleven-volume leather-bound collection. In retro-spect I see them as the screams of every man who ever screamed as whatever pain had been visited on him laid siege to his courage, his strength, his senses, and his faith.

At first he lay on his back and no matter what the medic did the kid's probing and pinching and pushing hands went back to the wound, his fingers like those of a blind man trying to learn how to type. He would rip the compress off, thrust his fingers into his guts, and pull them out again bloody and wet. Gently, he tried to lay the serrated flaps of skin back in place to close up the hole. Then he would rub it in a small cir-cle, as if this would make the torn skin reseal. The circle would be described by his bloody fingers faster and harder until he was pulling and tearing at his own skin, angrily trying to open it up again, stuffing parts A, B, and C back into con-tainer D. A place for everything and everything in its place. While he did this he stared with bulging eyes at the gray and gauzy clouds beyond the reaching canopy, and screamed.

The act of screaming for him was very physical. His shoul-ders gave him firm purchase against the ground as he arched his back and dug in with his heels, lifting his hips up. Then he thrust his jaw forward as he tilted his head and neck back, al-lowing his mouth to stretch open to the max, his lips pulled and compressed against his straining teeth, his tongue S-curled and wiggling. Then, up and out from his throat, his gored belly, his lungs, his spine, his soul, would come the scream. It was a roar of shearing wind, all the fingernails of every deformed and twisted demon who had ever tormented Christ raked again and again across the chalkboard of rea-son. He brought it up and spit it out at the night, at us, at the jungle, at the scum-sucking coward Commie punk asshole motherfucker who had shot him and run away, and at his Maker.

Were they screams of pain only? No way. There was too much substance, too much depth to them. They were layered and textured, his screams, and they came to their richness in his *knowing*. He knew he was gut-shot and dying. *Why?* Why, he wanted to know. Why *can't* I be medevaced by this most modern and well-equipped army in the history of man? Back home on TV you tell my mom and all the moms that within ten minutes of "getting hurt" on the battlefield a soldier can receive first-class medical treatment because of the choppers and radios. So what am I, some fucking orphan child, some asshole who hasn't paid his dues? Some kid soldier who has no mom back in the World to impress? Why? Why wasn't one of the *other* guys hit with that bullet? Why *me*? Why did we have to come here, why is LBJ the fucking president, who the fuck *is* LBJ? Why couldn't that enemy soldier have had a jam in his crappy AK? Where in the living *fuck* is my piece-of-shit guardian angel? Who the hell gave *it* the day off? For that matter, where is my loving God? Been hearing all about you since I was a kid. This the kind of shit you let happen to all of us little children you love as your own son? What about my car? My car . . . you know, the badass GTO I was gonna get when I got home from this bullshit Vietnam? How am I gonna get that GTO now? Who's gonna tell my *mom*? What about the *girls*, goddammit? I've only been with one girl *one* time in my whole life . . . jackknifed into the backseat of my buddy's Chevy. I got to suck on one of her nipples, got her panties pulled to the side, and got my poor hard-on wedged in there long enough to have officially *made* it. But is that *it*? I never get to be with an entirely naked girl? Never get to spend the night with one, never get to *taste* one? What about a wife, kids, school, a job, a *life*? What about an electric guitar, what about surfing? What about my dreams, god-dammit . . . what about my *dreams*?

Most of us forgot the jungle, forgot the enemy, forgot stupid Vietnam and the stupid war. We were just *there*, locked into that night with his screams. Where could we go? We were in the jungle, in fucking Southeast piece-of-shit Asia with his chewing and burning screams. We hunkered down, waiting it out. Either he would tire himself, the drugs would shut him up, morning would come, or—fuck, yeah, I'll say it—or that bad boy in black, that bony-handed skull-headed doomsday-fucking dream-ruiner Grim Reaper could come gliding through our perimeter, snag his howling gut-shot carcass, and take him the hell *out* of there.

Finally, when you thought he'd have to be tiring, his screams would have to fade, he'd have to trail off into some kind of oblivion, the belly-wounded kid sat up. The medic tried to push him down, but the kid sat up, looked at the mess in his hands, put his head back so his searching eyes could look into the disdainful sky where rumor has it heaven is, and screamed. He got into a rhythm . . . scream, sccrreeaamm, scccrrreeeaaammm, *gulping breath, gulping breath,* scream . . .

Without coordinating the move, two or three guys at once rolled out of their holes and crawled to where the medic lay with the screaming guy. They jumped him, sprawling their bodies over his, hugging him, palming his face, hissing into his ear *Take it easy, It's okay, It's okay, Shut up, Shut the fuck up, Shut the fuck up you motherfucker, SHUTTHEFUCKUP YOUMOTHERFUCKERORISWEARI'LLKILLYOUMYSELF!* The medic, manically trying to stay by his charge, pulled and shoved at them with exhausted hands.

"Hit him with more juice, goddammit, hit him with more—"

"I *can't*. I already gave him way more. . . . It should have been enough to— I can't just fill him with morphine, it'll *kill* him—"

"Do something. Do *something*."

But there was nothing, and they knew it. They crawled back to their holes, two of them openly sobbing.

The kid continued to scream. Louder and louder he screamed, until there was no other reality.

With the very first hint of pink-streaked dawn came the throbbing beat of the approaching medevac chopper. With leaden hands and stumbling feet, seared and etched faces, dry mouths, rotting hearts, and weeping ears, we carried him to the chopper, slung into a green poncho, with his boots toe-bumping together as we walked, his legs limp and useless, the stench of his bowels filled our nostrils. His screams had died on that hill as he had died with the coming of day.

He tumbled onto the cold deck of the Huey in that loose and floppy way, and the medic was carefully helped aboard behind him. During the last mourning hours the medic had borrowed a black marker from me, and with it he had methodically painted over each lens of his Army-issue glasses. He was done now, done with it all, and we never saw him again.

We turned our backs as the chopper lifted off, our souls resembling the negatives of those who survived at the edge of Dresden and Hiroshima.

Prophylactic

I WAS a shiny new butterbar LT assigned to a self-propelled 155 battery squatting on Highway 19. I was trying to learn how to be a strong leader, and an officer the men knew was fair and responsive to their needs and perceptions. The battery commander was stuck with me in this static position, and in the army young LT's must be kept busy. The good captain, out of either desperation or malice, conferred upon me the title of Vice Officer.

"Tell the men about the clap, Lieutenant," said the captain briskly. "Tell them not to ride bareback. Tell them to stay away from the whores. Tell them the whores are usually VC spies and infiltrators, and while they are in our perimeter they compromise security and give their VC leaders info so they can accurately mortar us. Understood?"

"Yes sir."

"You shouldn't have too much to worry about right now, Lieutenant," he continued. "I mean, with the whores in our perimeter. I've given *strict* orders to the first sergeant to put out the word, *No more whores*, so there are no whores here to worry about at this time. Understood?"

"Yes sir."

A sultry rain fell as I stood there responding to the captain's instructions. Everything was gray and brown and muddy, all the men, guns, and equipment soaked by the continuous warm drizzle. As the captain went on I glanced over his shoulder at a group of soldiers walking out of some bunkers on the far side of the perimeter. The soldiers were leaving the bunkers and heading for the barbed-wire gate that protected the road. There were four of them, and even to my untrained eye they looked like the smallest American soldiers I had ever seen. Their diminutive stature was accentuated by the tin-pot army helmets precariously balanced on their small heads, and the slick-wet puke-green ponchos that covered their slight bodies. Oddly enough, the soldiers did not have their delicate feet shod in clunky boots, but rather wore cheap rubber shower sandals in the mud. I saw one turn back toward the bunkers and smile and wave at a shirtless trooper at the entrance. He grinned back. Then the little huddle of Munchkin-like wraiths, in their ponchos and helmets, disappeared into the mist.

"Understood?" repeated the captain.

"Yes sir," said I.

An hour later I was accosted by a soldier who would become my RTO.

"You heard about my reputation, LT?" he asked.

"Uh—"

"You know, LT—about me and the girls in this country? About how they *love* my ass?"

"Uh, no . . . Well . . . It's possible I may have heard—"

"Listen, LT," said the soldier, "I ain't shittin' ya, this is one completely fucked country we're fightin' in here, but the *women* . . . the women are unbelievable. *Nice*, even the whores, LT. Like, most of 'em got small little titties and are skinny, so if you're a boob man your hands feel kinda empty. But man, can they *screw*."

"Good. Right. We are, uh, expected to find the *good* things about our hosts' culture—"

"No shit, LT. Anyway, I thought you might have already heard about my reputation with these girls here. Hell, I see by your expression you ain't. Listen. You see those bunkers over there? That's where my squad lives for now. Wait about fifteen minutes, LT, then walk over there nice and easy and come inside. I'll be there with a *friend*, and I want you to see me in action."

"Yes. Um, no . . . uh, *thank you*, soldier, but I'm not sure it would be—"

"Whatsamatter, LT? You one of these fuckin' ring-knockers we got runnin' around out here tryin' to *lead* us, but don't want to know nothin' *about* us?"

"Fifteen minutes. I got it."

Sure enough, his *friend* was there. At first all I could see were the soles of her feet glowing in the gloom of the soggy bunker, then parts of her legs, one arm, and eventually her face. She was very slight, completely naked, and looked young but with an old expression. I saw plenty of my RTO's shining white posterior bouncing up and down, then his grinning face as he turned and huffed at me, "Hey, LT, thanks for showing up. You see this little thing I'm ridin' here? Is she a cutie, or what?"

"Certainly. Uh, *yes* . . . very . . . cute . . ."

"You checkin' my *style*, LT? You see me *drivin'*? Shit, I'm makin' this little whore *crazy*. She probably won't even charge me full price."

"Uh . . ."

"Wanted you to see this, LT. Wanted you to see me in action so when you heard about my reputation you'd understand."

I had the feeling he wanted to say more, but then his breathing changed and he began huffing and puffing, and I turned to get out of there. Over his left shoulder the girl's face hung in the gloom. She held an apple in the hand I could see, and she brought it to her smiling mouth, took a big bite, and winked at me. I left.

And, wouldn't you know it, we *were* mortared that night.

Night Sweats

YEAH, there's lots of shit flyin' around, our artillery, your mortars, your green tracers and our orange ones. Lots of small-arms stuff, machine-gun *tacha-tacha-tacha*, and the whoosh-*bang* of your rocket-propelled grenades. You opened up on the truck convoy again, huh, tryin' to cut the lines of supply to Dak To. You gonna blow up a couple of trucks and cut the lines, Charles? Don't you know how we build trucks back home, the numbers? You don't have a clue, but here you sprung it anyway, and now the shit is comin' *down* and the hot steel is flyin' and tearin' and at least one truck is burnin' and guys are screamin', and you and your compatriots are charging out of the tree line, shooting as you come.

I'm in my jeep, my Recon driving us north behind the convoy as fast as we can go. I don't have to be out here on the highway to do my thing with the ARTY. I can sit back, use my all-powerful radios, and bring the shit down on your sorry ass, your tree line, your jump-off and gathering points, and your likely routes of egress. But no . . . I *want* to be part of this fight. My Recon thinks I'm a dumbass LT who should know better, but he sets his jaw and drives us out here anyway.

I'm sitting on the right side of the jeep, my M-14—we didn't have the M-16 yet—pointed at the floorboards between my legs. I been here almost six months, and this is my third or fourth roadway ambush, right? No matter. We're bumping through the dust and smoke, the radios are goin' crazy, and we can see some of your buddies off in the haze, running toward the road from the tree line, running and falling, running and falling.

Now, out of the corner of my eye, I see you. Why you waited, I don't know. The bulk of the convoy is long gone up the road, and here I come now in my little jeep. Did you see the radio antennas, is that it? You see those antennas and think I'm worthy of your attention, worthy of that RPG you're carrying in the launcher high up on your right shoulder as you run? You come out of the scrub beside some felled trees, your sandal-shod feet churning dust as you run in a half-crouch toward us through the loose dirt.

Look at you. Why, you look like a fucking *recruitment* poster for the NVA. You got your green-on-green uniform, your tan rucksack, your dusty-green pith helmet with red star. Even got a red star on your flat metal belt buckle. Got yourself a fresh haircut, too, didn't you? Yes sir, that comes from your wily leaders, huh—the haircut thing? They want us to see how squared-away you are, how unfazed by your trip south, those months on the Ho Chi Minh Trail and in the bowels of the jungle. That's why you always got your bullshit fresh haircut when you come out to fight, so we'll be impressed. Well . . . I'm impressed, okay?

I see how you begin to slow your run now, only fifty meters from my jeep. You slow so you can take better aim with your RPG. And you're aiming it at *me*. But I've got my good old M-14 with a full magazine of 7.62mm jacketed rounds. It's a solid weapon, much like the heavy M-1 my uncle Steve carried, tough and dependable. I'm gonna bring it up now and begin shooting it at you before you launch that fucking rocket and blow us up.

Except the barrel of my M-14 won't come up. Wait, *wait*. I see you begin to kneel now, your face a mask of concentration as you put me in your sights. *Wait*, you son of a bitch, my goddamned M-14 won't come up, it feels like it weighs more than this piece-of-shit jeep. *Dammit*, maybe this is one of those slo-mo dream sequences where you know you're about to die and you can't squeeze the trigger or your leaden legs won't move or you can't lift the barrel of your weapon. I hear my Recon yelling, Shoot, *shoot* him . . . *Shoot the bastard*. But my damn barrel won't come up. It has picked this moment to become afflicted with a deadly impotency.

You become very still, and point the business end of your RPG at my face—*right at my face*—and all I can see besides the fading green you is the big black hole that is the tip of the green prick bulbous-nose rocket. *Fuck you I'm gonna look down and see what the hell is wrong with the end of my barrel*.

Oh.

The front sight is caught under the edge of the instrument panel of the jeep. All I have to do is pull it back slightly, then lift it up and out. Now I swing it toward you and begin squeezing them off, squeezing and stroking that perfect little trigger. *Blam*, I don't see it. *Blam*, I see the bullet rip up the dirt a few feet to your right. *Blam*, it takes you in the chest . . . *blam, blam, blam*.

Rise up now, motherfucker. *Fuck yeah*! Stagger up and back as my *for sure* rounds punch into your shit-assed NVA poster-child torso. Go ahead now, squeeze it off, squeeze off that rocket . . . *WHOOSH* . . . too late. You waited too long while I dicked around with the barrel of my M-14. Now you've fired your farting rocket right over my fucking *head*, you stupid bastard. Look at it. *Look at it*, over us and out of sight into the other tree line. Gone, baby, it's *gone*, but I'm still here and I'm still *shooting* and now you jump and spin and writhe around, motherfucker. Now you *die* as you fling the empty tube into the dirt, as your oh-so-Jane pith helmet falls away from your shitbird psychological haircut, as your bowels open and fill your green pants, as your heels beat a tattoo into the dirt. Now you *die*, you son of a bitch.

"Holy *shit*!" I hear my Recon yell as if in a dream, as he straightens our jeep and jams the gears to roar north after the convoy. *"Holy shit, did you see that dink motherfucker try to kill us?"*

I say nothing; I have no spit. My hands grip the M-14 too tightly to shake.

"God *damn*," comes Recon's voice. "I thought you'd *never* shoot that bastard." He wipes his face with one hand. "Motherfucker tried to *kill* us."

I say nothing.

Equation

Most of us were not career soldiers, but we could learn the intricacies of our craft well enough to be efficient and to survive. There may have been many things we did not understand about our enemy, but it did not take us long to recognize his tactics. We had after-action summaries, intelligence reports, POW's to listen to, former members of VC or NVA cadres who defected to our side and taught us, and our own experiences.

Their squad- and platoon-level leaders interested me, the way they fought, the way they thought. There was a certain part of their ambush tactics I wanted to explore, to see if I could get into the way they thought, get into their heads.

"Watch what happens," the leader of the NVA ambush squad told his men before placing them. "Let their first soldier get within a few yards, then fire your weapons low. The first soldier will go down." He paused, shook his head, and added, "Then watch what they do . . . and stay prepared to shoot more."

The NVA leader set his men very carefully. Their position was in the deep forest-jungle west and north of Pleiku, in the highlands: triple canopy, lush and beautiful. He picked a spot where the trail began to rise up the gentle slope of a ridge-line, where both sides fell away sharply into cluttered ravines, where the tangled and twisted leaves and vines limited visibility to a few yards. The sites for his men were in natural cover; several small trails led over the ridgeline for escape. From these positions his men looked down on anyone approaching.

Private Smith walked point. Back in the World he was a pudgy college guy interested in Renaissance literature; here he was a rangy and tired American soldier interested in making it through the day. He was aware that the trail was an old one, saw no sign of recent use, but stayed alert because of the terrain. He didn't like it that the trail began to rise slightly beneath his boots. It was a gentle rise, but having to scan *up* into the green made him uncomfortable. Something about the green didn't feel right, anyway, and as he put one hand up to halt the men behind him, his legs and lower torso were hammered by punching incoming rounds. As he twisted and fell he heard the roar of the ambush being sprung, and he fired his weapon in a long burst into the jungle as the pain seared him and the spongy earth slapped the side of his face. He dropped his rifle, tucked into the fetal position, and grabbed his bleeding legs.

"Point's *down*! Point's *down*!"

The men behind Smith lay in a ragged line on the trail, blindly firing their weapons over his writhing form into the dense jungle growth where the enemy fire came from. Only one or two could fire because of how they lay.

"Get some ARTY up, give us some ARTY."

"*Medic! Medic!*"

"Tell the LT we can't move to the right or left because of the way this fuckin' trail slopes down into that ravine. . . ."

Booommm.

"*Fuck*—the ravine is booby-trapped, the ravine is booby-trapped."

"*Medic! . . .*"

Now the Americans began to act in the way the NVA leader found so odd, the way he wanted his men to see and learn. Jones came first. He was just a grunt rifleman, a skinny kid with unruly rust-colored hair and a pimply chin. He had worked in the produce section of a supermarket back home. He wasn't even great friends with Smith, the wounded point. He was just a grunt rifleman. But he lay there on the trail, cowering under the solid roar of hot flying metal and explosions, saw Smith was hurt but still alive twenty feet in front of him, and shrugged out of his pack. He grabbed his M-16, fired a long burst into the green above the wounded point man's body, and lunged forward.

It was exactly what the NVA leader had told his men would occur. The NVA soldiers had continued to fire in steady but economical bursts after the first American went down on the trail; they were largely untouched by the American return fire, which expended itself in the jungle. They waited to see if— *There*, just as their leader had predicted, another American was moving up, moving toward the first one. They let him come.

*　　*　　*

Jones got to Smith, rolled the grimacing point man toward him, then was slammed down to the dirt of the trail by the first impacting NVA bullets which knocked his helmet off his head and sent it spinning into the bushes, exploded one canteen on his hip, and punched into his chest and shoulder. Jones screamed, bolted up, took one more round in the throat, and fell across Smith.

"*Slim went down!* Oh goddammit Slim went down tell the LT Slim went down too!"

"*Medic. . . !*"

"How long until we get some artillery on that ridge?"

"ARTY's being adjusted now. . . ."

"*Fan out!* Fan out even if you have to edge down into that ravine on the side of the trail." Pause. "*Watch for tripwires.*"

"Get some fire up the trail. . . . Get some fire into the base of the ridgeline. . . . Get some fire out. . . . *Shoot, shoot, shoot* . . ."

Boom.

"That one of our grenades, or mortars?"

"LT, we got two men down on the trail."

"Get some 79 onto that ridge. . . . Where's the bloop gunner?"

Boom. Boom.

Now the NVA gunners understood what their leader wanted them to see. They hunkered down grimly in their fighting holes, sensing the increase in the volume of incoming American fire, feeling and hearing the impact of the hated American artillery crashing behind them, but determined to hang on for a few more minutes. *They won't leave their dead or wounded*, their leader had told them, *no matter how indefensible their position.* There are no nearby areas for their helicopters to come for them, and it takes *four* able soldiers to carry out one wounded, two for a dead one. The NVA leader had told them what to look for next.

"*Medic!* Where's Doc?"

Before Doc could crawl up the narrow trail, Brown shed *his* pack and his helmet, turned to Miller lying hugged up against his legs, and croaked through a parched throat, "My mama *told* me there'd be days like this."

Miller looked at him with bulging eyes and croaked back, "What you gonna *do*, nigger?" But his friend gave him what he thought was a confident grin, grunted as he lifted himself to his knees, and charged forward up the trail toward the wounded Smith and Jones.

The NVA machine-gunner thought his eyes were playing tricks on him in the shadows of the jungle when he saw Brown crouching and lunging toward the first two Americans. The machine-gunner had never seen a man so big, Caucasian *or* Negro, and he was fascinated by how white Brown's teeth and eyes looked against his wet-shiny black skin. He let the American Negro soldier get up against the other two, waited until the big man hunched to his knees to pull them apart, then fired a long searing burst into their huddle.

With painless clarity Brown knew his right kneecap had exploded into shards and fragments as the bullet ripped it away. With the same clarity he knew the other bullets that hit him, one in the right thigh, the last in his left hip, would not kill him. Using his bulk and the flak jacket he wore, he rolled his body in front of the other two: they had been hit again by the fire. As he rolled he threw the grenade he had been holding in his right hand, threw it into a dark hole in the foliage where he thought the machine-gun fire came from. Then he hunched tight with his nostrils in the dirt of the trail, his eyes squeezed shut.

The NVA machine-gunner saw the Negro soldier throw something, and when the grenade thudded into the dirt in front of his position he couldn't believe it. He had turned his head to ask his assistant gunner if *he* saw it, when his whole world became a rocking flashing burning roar, and he was knocked back against the trunk of a tree, the hot and bent remains of his gun wrapped in his shredded arms. He was going to ask his assistant gunner if he saw *that*, but his eyes finally focused enough to see his assistant beside him, bent forward as if praying, his legs covered with his intestines, his face buried in the mess.

"ARTY walking down—*heads down*—artillery coming down the ridgeline . . ."

"Doc . . . *Doc*—Smith, Jones, *and* Brown are hit. See them? I can't tell if they're still moving or not."

"I see 'em."

"Doc, *wait*—we think Brown got their MG, but there's still a *lot* of shit flying . . ."

"Doc, *Doc! Shit! Fire!* Shoot, shoot . . . Get some more fire over their heads!"

Boom. Boom.

"Goddammit . . . is that mortars or is somebody throwing grenades?"

The NVA leader had seen the first three Americans fall, knew one or two of his men had been hit, knew that somehow the Negro soldier had blown up his machine-gun team, knew the American artillery was falling closer with each adjustment, but wanted his men to see one more thing. *There*. In spite of how hard it was to believe, there came one more American: a *doctor*-soldier who walked with the common soldiers. A doctor-soldier who didn't even carry a rifle and who would . . .

Jesus Huerta, nicknamed Doc Hurt-ya, was a roly-poly caramel-skinned open-faced kid from Miami, Florida. He was a good guy from a tough neighborhood who might have been a priest. He felt it would not be right to avoid the draft, even though the war in Vietnam was so obviously stupid, but he told the Army he had no intention of killing anyone. They trained him as a medic, which secretly pleased him very much, and he worked hard to give whatever care he could to the men in his outfit. He belly-crawled up the trail to the three wounded men as the roar of the firefight filled the green.

Doc sensed the increased volume of fire coming from both directions. As he grabbed Jones, who was draped over Smith, he pulled Jones by the collar and dragged him back down the trail a few feet. He knew immediately that Jones was dead, but checked vitals quickly anyway. He turned from him as he saw other hands reaching for the limp body. He pulled his face close against Smith's, heard the ragged breaths, then said in a surprisingly normal voice, "Hey, Brown . . . can you move on your own?"

"Yeah," responded the big black soldier.

"Okay," continued Doc, "I'll drag Smith, you crawl with us. What about if we just roll off into the ravine?"

"I'm afraid of booby traps, Doc," grunted Brown through his pain. "Plus, I don't know how far we'd roll."

Doc nodded. Then he began to pull Smith backward down

the trail. Brown slid in the soft wet dirt with him, inch by inch under the hail of fire. "Only a few more feet," said Doc. "I think their fire is tapering off." He flinched as a bullet cut the skin of his left cheek.

The NVA leader had already given the signal. His men were quickly withdrawing, their preplanned routes taking them over the ridgeline and through another draw that kept them out of the artillery fire. He was surprised at the loss of three men, but left their bodies where they lay. He had been taught to remove the bodies of his fallen whenever possible, to deny the Americans any tangible signs of success. He did not feel it was possible today, and actually felt some urgency to leave the area as quickly as he could. He shouldered past a couple of his men pushing through the green. Still, he thought the battle and the lesson had gone well.

The Americans were poor soldiers, noisy, frightened, and ill-disciplined, and almost every time they came under attack they would multiply their casualties by four. How incredibly stupid.

Grunt's Soliloquy

"**Q**UIT crowdin' my ass. The LT said to watch our spacing."

"Fuck the LT, fuck this trail, fuck this hump . . . and fuck the Army."

"Gee, that was original."

"Do you mean in the literal sense?"

"If you can't say something nice . . ."

"Where are we *going*?"

"Why do *you* wanna know? Writing a book?"

"We're humping the trail, just like we do every god-damned day out here in the boonies."

"Yeah, but to *where*? I mean, what is our objective?"

"Man wants to know what is our objective."

"No shit? You gotta be kidding."

"Hey, shit-for-brains, listen up. We're humping this trail in the boonies, got it? Does it look like the same thing we did yesterday? It is. Yesterday our *objective* was a ville, remember?

We walked the trail until we got close to the ville; then the Viet Cong—you remember *them*?—a bunch of angry young patriots intent on wastin' your ass? Then the VC *shot* at us as we approached their little ville. Then the LT, the very same LT who told us to watch our spacing today, he got on his little radio—he don't *hump* it, but he *talks* on it—and he called down a bunch of shit onto that little ville. When the boomin' and crashin' was done there was nothin' left in the ville 'cept a couple of frantic chickens and a few scared villagers hidin' in their filthy family bunker. We dug them out, screamed at 'em some, then burned what was left of the ville down to ashes with our Zippos. Got it?"

"Yeah, I got it, but you forgot to mention what happened when the young and patriotic Viet Cong shot at our sorry asses."

"Fuck."

"Yeah. Anderson got shot in the balls."

"Not *in* the balls, *through* the balls."

"So what? *In* the balls, *through* the balls—fucked him up, man. Had to medevac his ass. Doc couldn't hardly get him out of that twisted fetal position long enough to load him onto the chopper."

"Yeah. When Doc first cut open his pants to see the wound, old Anderson looked down through his fingers and said, 'Oh shit . . . looks like I'm *permanently* on the rag.'"

"You heard him say that? All I heard was him screamin' and yellin' and Doc sayin' it was all right because he still had his *dick*—"

"What good is a dick with no balls?"

"I don't know."

"Me neither."

"Got me."

"Uh-huh . . ."

"Well, either way, I think because of what happened to Anderson, I think that's why the LT called in the artillery and air strikes and all that shit onto the ville. That's why he tol' us to burn it. The LT was really pissed off about Anderson gettin' shot in the balls."

"Do LT's have balls?"

"Asshole."

"I *know* they have assholes. . . . Aw, forget it."

"Hey, you guys. Yesterday there was Anderson's balls and the burnt ville. *My* question is where are we going *today*?"

"Holy shit."

"Man's dumber than a post."

"One more time. We are humping this trail today, watching our spacing and supposedly maintaining good noise discipline. Humping along through the jungle, over the ridgeline, beside the rice paddy, and we are going to *another ville*."

"But *why*?"

"To win the hearts and minds of the people."

"But, dammit. It all looks the same—the same as yesterday. The trail looks the same, the jungle looks the same, you and the rest of the guys look the same, the LT, the sky, the choppers, the ville, the people *in* the ville, the chickens, the flies, the shit floating in the rice paddy, the elephant grass, the sweat, the back of the guy's neck in front of me . . . it's the same."

"So?"

"So what is our fucking objective?"

"Your objective, numb-nuts, is not to get your balls shot off."

Drumbeat

IT wasn't like Little Big Horn. It wasn't like D Day, the Charge of the Light Brigade, Iwo Jima, Chosin, the Somme, Dunkirk, Gettysburg, Kuwait, or the Alamo. It was more like a bar fight, a slugfest, a vicious brawl between two tough pissed-off guys in a small space. My old man told me about a style of knife fighting where the two combatants each placed one foot on a handkerchief on the floor, foot-to-foot, both grabbed another handkerchief with one hand and pulled tight, then went at each other with the knife they held in the other hand. Tight, quick, and bloody. It was like that.

They knew the lay of the land, and before they lost so many soldiers to attrition they were veterans—tough, dedicated, and experienced. The Viet Cong fought on their home turf, and the NVA were guided by the VC. Many of them had years of combat experience, an undivided ruling cadre with a single long-range vision, and no way to get out except to be dead or cripple-wounded.

We were young, came from an affluent and soft society,

and had no clear direction or motivation. Many of us had been drafted to fight in a war we knew was wrong or at least misguided. Many of us had become soldiers for the adventure; we were ignorant of the cultural and political landscape. We were part-time soldiers with no real stake in the land or the outcome. We were led by other youngsters schooled in leadership and constantly rotated out of the combat zone just about the time they began to benefit from the experience. But—and this is a "but" the North Viet leadership failed to understand—we came from a country founded on, nurtured by, respectful of, and fascinated by war.

It could be argued that in many respects the quick brutal firefights in Vietnam were simply an extension of the parking lot fistfights that took place back in the World during our high school years. Maybe "gang fight" would be a better word—but gang fights are usually about turf and/or honor. In Vietnam we rarely stayed on the turf we took, and it was difficult to find any honor associated with the South Viets we were trying to help. Basically we went out into the countryside looking for a fight, and if the VC or NVA were in the area and thought they could hurt us they'd open the festivities. They liked to get tight with us, draw us in close where we'd be hesitant to call in our incredible firepower. They liked to be in good defensive positions and catch us out in the open. They liked to surprise us, get us where we were most vulnerable, hurt us, and then hurt us more when we tried to get our hurt out.

We didn't like any of it. But that doesn't mean we didn't fight.

We were a strange, awkward, unpredictable, and dangerous bunch, all told. The VC and NVA soldiers often learned this the hard way by our response. Despite our lack of battle experience, our soft backgrounds, our lack of commitment or ideals, our always-new leaders . . . despite all that we quickly became a terrible force in the face of fire. It often happened where *they* wanted it to, when *they* wanted, and we would go down, we would be hit, we would fall and scream and beg for the medic. We would hunker down paralyzed with fear as the bullets tore and the mortars crunched and the grenades boomed and ripped. We would writhe there in the carefully constructed kill zone and take it.

Until we didn't. Then they would look at us from their strong bunker dug into the cool, behind their Russian machine gun, safe from our air strikes and most of our artillery, and see us begin to . . . move. We wanted our wounded and our dead back in the fold. We wanted our wounded away from their gunners, who continued to fire at them, and after some undefined number of seconds passed while we hugged Mother Earth we would realize that in order to get our wounded we first had to get *them*. Some soldier from Tulsa would throw a grenade at the bunker. Another from Maine would fire a burst from his M-16. Some wise guy from New York would lean up just far enough to loose an antitank rocket into the fire, and two or three more from who the hell knows where would get up on their knees, then on their feet, and they would *move forward*, shooting as they went.

I wonder how many VC and NVA soldiers died as they stared in wonder at the awkward, ragtag, ill-led, unmotivated, soft, unprofessional soldiers coming to kill them.

As an aside: back in the World, after the fistfight was over the two combatants might wipe their bloody noses, grin, shake hands, and share a couple of beers.

Vietnam was not the World, and never will be.

Gastronomic

SHE was already famous for having sent a three-layer birthday cake to her oldest son. That's her oldest son stationed at Fort Dix, New Jersey, in the middle of Advanced Infantry Training, guided in his lessons by a determined group of very serious Drill Instructors. The three-layer cake was baked, but in a disassembled state when it arrived during mail call, so her oldest son was faced with the daunting task of putting it together *and* surviving the jibes of his barracks-mates and the wrath of the DI's. Fortunately, the DI's simply walked away shaking their heads and muttering about the old days, and the barracks-mates helped out with the building *and* eating of the cake.

Her reputation was lifted to mythical status when she managed to ship *three five-gallon cans* full of goodies from the World to her oldest son stationed in Viet-holy-shit-what-I'd-give-for-a-can-of-Vienna-sausages-or-a-real-Hershey-Bar-*Nam*. The man at her local post office told her to expect only one-third of her shipment to actually make it to the recipient in Vietnam, so she packed and shipped three. All three made it.

It was unbelievable. I was the wealthiest man on the planet, with tons of hard candy, toothpaste, writing stuff, toilet stuff, gigantic Hershey Bars, gum, Vienna sausages, pepperoni, playing cards, M&M's—goodies, goodies, goodies. Had so much I invited my friend Dave from a couple of klicks away to bring his guys and come over. He did. They brought a football. The ARVN's sat around watching the game, not understanding the nuances but taking great glee in the sight of the big clumsy Americans smashing into each other while fighting for possession of an inflated pig. Nor could they believe the goodies and the open generosity with which we shared them. All who were there that day agreed I was the oldest son of an incredible mom.

I received another package from the World once, after having been assigned to the indigenous troops for a month or so. I had been with ARVN, Special Forces, and Montagnard units throughout the Central Highlands, eating C-rats, Lurp-rations, rice-and-veggies, rice-and-goat, rice-and-dog, rice-and-mystery-meat, and the always popular fish-heads-and-rice. I was in the boonies when the package from the World arrived, and since it was shoe-box size I figured it contained goodies. Yessir, I could not wait, so I sat down on the trail after the resupply chopper chugged away, and ripped into it, my mouth already watering at the thought of *real good stuff from the World.*

It was from a friend. It was something called a Double-O Seven Survival Pack. It contained dried snake meat. It contained deep-fried honey-dipped locusts. It contained chocolate-covered ants, dehydrated snails, something called

Nightcrawler Paste, flattened octopus tentacles, and what appeared to be a plastic bag filled with various-size eye-balls.

I left it beside the trail for the NVA, and went off looking for some fish-heads-and-rice.

Microcosm

WHILE conducting my recon-by-fire when I went back into the green, I searched for a battle illustrative of many. My memory took me back to one particular dawn, when I—a smooth-faced LT at the time—walked the perimeter of an outpost that had come under attack during the night. It was an unheralded incident of combat, fought over time and terrain soon forgotten. The units engaged were representative of both sides; the men involved could have been found anywhere in Vietnam during the war.

Young officers learn to pay attention to the verbalizations of the troops, and I captured bits and pieces of conversation when I could. I knew their feelings, understood their prejudices, and shared their frustrations and fears. The enemy structures were known to us, as were their methods of attack and their unit philosophies—and with the dawn you could stand in the wire and see the shape of their attack in the bodies left behind.

This was part of my war, but not my battle. I was there,

but on the edges, and it swept around me like a thunder-storm, gone with the sun. At the same time it became *the* moment of pure combat for other men—it was their fight, their battle, their war—and I wanted to preserve it. But from a respectful distance.

Huu Cao. Tran Van Duc. Xuan Minh.

Three young men from North Vietnam, one a farmer, one a student, one a small-appliance repairman. That's what they used to be before they joined the Righteous Struggle to Free the Homeland from the Tyrannic Oppressors. Now they were soldiers in the North Vietnamese Army—the PAVN, People's Army of Vietnam. Now they were a cell, a three-man Communist cell. The three-man cell was designed and implemented by the Communist leaders to ensure that each soldier had a built-in support system. Each soldier *always* had someone with him, during training, indoctrination, times of rest and personal hygiene, and battle. Each of the three helped watch over the other two, helped the other two absorb and comprehend the doctrines taught, helped the other two cope with the hardships and trials associated with being patriots, helped the other two stay the course. Each of the three reported on the other two, also, to ensure there were no slackers, no cancerous free thoughts, to ensure there was unity. The three-man Communist cell made no room for the individual.

Cao, Duc, and Minh ate, slept, and trained together. They learned how to use the vaunted AK-47 assault rifle, the B-40 rocket-propelled grenade, and the hand grenades, both Chinese and American. They were shown the satchel charge, the small mortar, and the basics of booby-trapping. They learned the signals by which the leaders would tell them to form up for battle after they made their way to the jump-off line.

They practiced their assigned tasks for the assault: Cao to cut the wire after the mortars lifted, Duc to fire the B-40 into the specified enemy position, and Minh to charge forward followed by his cellmates, firing his AK from the hip. The hated Americans were soft, the three were taught, soft and confused and racially divided and messed up on dope. They would sit behind their defensive wire waiting for their powerful artillery and airplanes to win the battle for them. But, the three-man cell was taught, the artillery and air strikes would come too late to save them, for the three-man cell and all the other three-man cells making up the battalion of freedom fighters would already be through the wire and among them, shooting, killing, and taking prisoners.

The Americans wanted to show the impressionable people of the villages that they controlled the countryside, the three-man cell was taught. So the Americans built the company-sized assault and resupply compound in the light jungle bordering the rich ricelands. Now it was up to the freedom fighters to display to the villagers just how misguided the Americans were. Using a battalion to attack a defending company, the classic four-to-one ratio, the Communist battalion would overrun the compound, kill and destroy, take prisoners, run the PAVN flag up the pole, and disengage before dawn, leaving destruction and a defeated enemy behind.

The three-man cells would be the fighters who would make it happen. People's Soldiers Huu Cao, Tran Van Duc, and Xuan Minh . . . they were the ones.

The men in the company-size outpost cut into the low hills bordering the rice paddies and backed by the mountains watched the sunset that evening with a feeling of dread. There had been no overt signal of impending attack, no captured prisoner with the exact time and date on his lips, no crisp and starched major from Division Intelligence with satellite, sensor, infrared, or sniffer info hot off the presses. The surrounding villagers hadn't disappeared into the jungle—always a clear tip-off—because there *weren't* any surrounding villagers. Civilians who used to live in the region had been "relocated," courtesy of the government. Anyone there now was the enemy.

And the enemy had been out and about during the last week. He had stepped up his patrols, he had dug carefully camouflaged gun pits in a half-circle around the compound, he had left trail markers so his soldiers could find their way in the dark, and he had probed twice on previous evenings. One probe consisted of a few mortar rounds dropped almost haphazardly around the wire. With these he hoped to gauge the depth and time of the American counterbattery fire, and to register his own fire for attack. The second probe was a deliberate push into the wire by a squad of sappers to check its integrity. They were quickly repulsed, leaving behind the body of a soldier that told the Americans a lot. The body was that of a man who was healthy and fit, with new equipment, full uniform, and Eastern-bloc ammo. He was not a local Viet Cong, part-time soldier. He had traveled from the North with a well-trained, well-equipped unit of the NVA, coming all that way perhaps for this specific assault on this specific American outpost. He would be from at least a company-size unit, more probably battalion-size, and they would have supporting arms such as mortars, heavy anti-aircraft machine guns, and possibly rockets. The body showed the Americans that their enemy approached in numbers, with planning, preparation, and determination.

What bothered the Americans most, besides their awareness of these signs, was the weather. Even though they weren't high in the mountains, the last couple of nights had been foggy, with low cloud cover. The fog came early in the evening hours and hung low until almost dawn, and that along with the clouds would restrict the use of flareships, gunships, and fighter-bombers in support. They could still call for prearranged artillery fire, and they had a four-deuce mortar in the compound, but each and every one of them felt more vulnerable to some degree without the Linus-blanket of promised or expected airpower.

Three of the American soldiers were ordered into a fighting hole fifteen meters from the inner edge of the wire. They didn't know the smooth-skinned shaky-voiced lieutenant who placed them there, they didn't know the soldiers in the fighting holes directly to their front between them and the wire, and they didn't know each other. One was from an artillery battery that had been pulled out a week ago. He had been sent back with three others to prepare the last of their gear to be lifted out. One was from the infantry company that called the compound home. And the last was from an engineer detachment sent to help build new bunkers. The cannon-cocker had been in-country five months, the grunt three months, and the shovel-shooter four days.

"Another clusterfuck," said Patrick O'Meara under his breath as the lieutenant walked away. "Here it is gettin' dark already and I've had one meal of C-rats all day and now I'm in this fuckin' hole with you two and every asshole on this hill knows Charlie's gonna hit us tonight."

"What are you," asked Bertrand Washington, "some kinda *ex*pert?"

"Maybe," replied O'Meara. "So what you gonna do . . . uh, *Washington* . . . shit your pants when Charlie fires his first shot?"

"I won't be shittin', I'll be *sittin'*. Sittin' right here in the bottom of this sorry hole until it be all over—"

"Oh, wow, that'll be a *big* help if we get our asses overrun."

"Fuck you, overrun. Look here, we on the *second* line of holes, you see that? Behind us is the mortar pit, over to our right is the M-60 machine-gun bunker anchorin' the line, and all strung in front of us are all them infantry boys behind their wire and foogas and claymores and shit. If there *is* a fight tonight, all we gotta do is lay down in this hole and let it happen. Won't need us, nuh-uh."

"You see the weather? Look at the fog, look at those clouds. We're alone out here. There ain't gonna be no air support."

"It's O'Meara, right? Look, O'Meara, worry about it if you want. Shoot your little M-16 if the shit starts, but don't look for me, 'cause I'll be snug down in the bottom of this hole. This ain't *my* war nohow. This is the *white* man's war against these here Viet-kinda peoples. And here all the brothers been brought over here to *fight* the war—"

"Oh, man. Washington, don't start all that black power bullshit in this hole. I don't wanna listen to it all night. It's bullshit and you know it. Back at base camp you and your brothers can wear your beads and do your little salute and strut around cryin' about bein' o-pressed and all that shit, but out here in the fuckin' *boonies* we are only just *soldiers* together, understand? Fucking Charlie is gonna come across that wire tonight and he ain't gonna give a rat's ass if you're black and I'm white and our little third man there is in-between. He's just gonna be lookin' for a fight."

"Fuck it," said Washington, "it's not *my* war."

"Uh, guys," said Hector Diaz cautiously, "a buddy of mine loaded me up with canned fruit before they choppered me out here, and to tell you the truth I'm so damned nervous I don't think I can even eat any of it. You want some?"

"Shit yeah."

"Fuckin' A."

It began during that expectant mystical-eerie time when shadows, vapors, illusions, and imaginary footfalls rule the senses. Those alert and experienced heard it begin before the others, heard the hollow *chuungk* sound of the NVA mortars being fired from behind the closest ridge, and knew. The rest found out when the first rounds began exploding all around the perimeter. Then shrill cries of "Incoming!" could be heard. The mortars were marched with precision through the wire, first across the line of fighting holes and bunkers, and then onto ammo and command bunkers scattered in the compound. Immediately following were the carefully sighted recoilless and rocket rounds, which hit on or near the larger bunkers—especially the command bunker with its ridgeback of radio antennas.

The three-man cell made up of Cao, Duc, and Minh crouched in the leafy scrub on the edge of the perimeter and watched the battle unfold exactly as their leaders had described. Their mortars and rockets were ripping and tearing at the Americans, and just as they always did the Americans fired off illumination rounds to help them see what was coming. Because of the cloud cover, either their flares hung too high to be effective or the light was diffused by the fog, only creating more shadows and confusion. It happened just as the three-man cell had been told. Now they heard the whistles even as they saw the first tracers from their machine-gun positions reaching out and punching into the American line. The Americans seemed to be responding fitfully, a few bursts of their weird orange tracer-fire coming from one hole, then more from a bunker. The whistles meant it was time to move.

Huu Cao used his elbows to pull himself forward in the classic low crawl into the first strands of American wire. His Kalashnikov was strapped across his back, the wire cutters in his hands. Duc and Minh crawled behind him. Their movements were practiced, choreographed; they were a *cell*. Cao used the cutters on several strands of wire, and saw in the light of explosions and flares that much of the wire was old and displaced or already blown into pieces by the mortars. This had been predicted. He surged forward. There was an enormous roar off to his right and he immediately comprehended it was one of the always-dangerous American claymores, but the path of its deadly shrapnel did not concern him. He crawled forward, cutting the occasional piece of wire, until he was only a few meters from the first American position. It was a low bunker, and from it came sporadic fire from what appeared to be two rifles. They would be M-16's, Cao knew, and he had been taught to signal Duc with the rocket only for a machine gun. While he thought about this there was an explosion in front of the position, and the two rifles fell silent. He moved forward.

"*Goddammit!*" yelled O'Meara. "I can't see a goddamned thing. There's too much smoke and shit."

"Keep your head down, you asshole!" yelled Washington.

"Should we shoot?" asked Diaz.

"Shoot *what*, kid?"

"Dammit, Washington. Stand up here and help me watch to see if any of 'em get through the wire—"

"Fuck you, O'Meara. I done tol' you where I'm spending the night, *down in this hole*."

"Aw . . . *man*."

"Shouldn't we shoot?" asked Diaz.

"Christ almighty, Diaz," said O'Meara through clenched

teeth, "we got to see somethin' to shoot *at*, unnerstand?" He turned his head to say something more to Washington, then flinched and screamed, "*FUCK!*" as an explosion shook their hole.

"*Look*, they got the goddamned machine-gun bunker, blew it all to hell. Don't see no movement in there at all. . . ."

"Get down, O'Meara, before they see us in here and get us next."

"Shouldn't we be shooting now?"

Cao, Duc, and Minh watched with awe and satisfaction as the rocket Duc fired from his shoulder roared straight and true right into the American machine-gun bunker, and Cao touched his cellmates lightly on their shoulders when they saw how the fire stopped coming from the gun. Duc had made a direct hit. It was working exactly as their leaders had told them. All around now were explosions, rifle and machine-gun fire, whistles, screams, yells—the booming roaring crashing frightening exhilarating pounding rush of battle—and they could see the surge was *forward*, the attack went *forward* into the American compound. Of course. They had been trained for this, they had been told how it would be, and it *was*. The soft Americans were not fighting anymore from their front holes, they were either dead or hiding. Many of the other cells were already through the wire, and dark figures could be seen here and there, running through the compound, fire their backdrop. It was time for Cao, Duc, and Minh to lift up their AK's, leap to their feet, and charge through the last strand of wire.

"We're gettin' our asses kicked," said Washington as he flinched and hunched his shoulders in response to another crashing explosion off to the left. He had the rim of his helmet over the top of the sandbag, his wide eyes surveying the scene around him. "I think they're through the wire. . . . O'Meara. I think they're through the wire."

"Nice of you to join us, Washington," replied O'Meara. "Hell, yeah they're through the wire. They're runnin' all over the place. Somebody's got to get that fucking machine gun goin' again—it's the only muscle on this side of the perimeter, the heaviest firepower we *got* over here." He lunged, paused, then said, "Dammit, that's the second grenade I've thrown out that didn't go off."

"Uh . . . I mean, excuse me, O'Meara," ventured Diaz as he stood beside Washington trying to get some moisture into his mouth, "the last two things you've thrown out of our hole have been cans of peaches in heavy syrup."

"Jesus Christ, O'Meara, you stupid paddy mick," said Washington.

"Fuck it."

"Should we shoot yet?" asked Diaz.

"*Yes,*" said Washington and O'Meara.

Cao, Duc, and Minh saw the muzzle flashes from the M-16's in the large fighting hole to their front. Minh lobbed a grenade.

Boom.

"Fuck! *Fuck!* I can't see. . . . Shit . . . You guys all right?" asked O'Meara. He rubbed his face, looked for blood on his hands, and said, "Wait, now I can see. It was just dirt. I think that was a grenade, did you see where it came from? We need to get that fuckin' machine gun goin'—"

"*I'm* okay," said Washington. Then he looked to his left. "*Shit,* they got the wetback."

Diaz, whose whole world had gone bright orange for a millisecond, then black, then gray, and now had returned to fuzzy focus, lay back in the hole, his helmet blown away, his hands and face bloody from a myriad of small shrapnel wounds. He still grasped his M-16, and used it to struggle to a standing position again. He changed magazines, saw with wonder that his bleeding fingers still worked and were not shaking too badly, and spit. Then, without turning his head to look at Washington, he said: "A wetback is a Mexican—most of the time. I'm from Puerto Rico, okay? You can call me a spic, a greaser, or a 'Rican . . . but don't call me no wetback. *¿Comprende?*"

"Why the fuck is everybody so *sensitive* nowadays?" asked O'Meara.

They fell quiet as they watched the battle rage around them. They had no contact with the other fighting holes; they did not know where their sergeant or LT was; and with the smoke, fog, and fire of battle swirling around them they began to feel very alone. When they saw what appeared to be enemy soldiers flitting in and out of the smoke they fired short bursts from their M-16's. Enemy tracer fire flared over their heads a few times, and the boom and crunch of enemy grenades made them duck and hunch their shoulders. So far no fire had come from their rear.

Diaz fired into the gloom again, emptied the magazine, and popped it out. He flinched when another grenade went off close to their hole, this time to his right and behind. Whoever threw it had overshot his target. He heard the big artilleryman grunt and the black soldier curse after the explosion, then fumbled around with a bandolier and pulled out the last magazine. "We're running out of ammo," he said, his tongue and teeth still feeling gritty, "and they're still running around all over the place. We've got to keep shooting."

"Man," said O'Meara in a tight voice, "the kid's right. We need more ammo, we need more firepower, we need more time. This fucking battle has only just *begun*." He paused, looked at Washington, and said quietly through clenched teeth, "We need to see if that M-60 is damaged, and if it's not then we need to get it over here and start puttin' out some steady fire."

Washington stared at him for a long moment, then beyond him where the machine-gun bunker lay dark and silent. "I'll cover you, O'Meara," he said. "You go get it."

"Can't," croaked O'Meara, and turned his hips slightly toward Washington. His fatigues were blackened and torn, the glaring white exposed skin of his waist, hip, and lower back pocked, shredded, and bloody. "That last Chi-Com grenade got me good. I can stand, but I don't think I can move very far."

The black soldier took in the severity of the wounds with one glance. He turned his head to the left and looked at Diaz a moment, saw the wide eyes, the bloody face. He looked back at O'Meara, nodded, and said "Dammit." Then he turned, hoisted himself waist up against the shallow back wall of the hole, swung his legs out, got to his knees, and lunged forward in a low run toward the machine-gun bunker.

Dawn burst upon them too quickly for the soldiers of the PAVN. Dawn brought a brooding daylight and the hungry American gunships and jet fighters. Dawn brought retreat, never mind what the leaders and political cadre said; dawn brought retreat.

For the Americans, dawn nudged up the hillside in a slovenly crawl, still wrapped in the smoky tatters of fog and gunpowder, turning white faces waxen, turning black-copper stains dark red. With the dawn came power, the deep-throated power of helicopter engines, the chatter of artillery observers on the radios. The Americans could now stand. They could climb up out of the dirt, stand and survey their torn hill, look down at their sueded combat boots and see the tread on them firmly dug into the *ground*. It was *their* ground while they chose to stay, *their* hill. *They* stood there, not the PAVN.

Huu Cao, Tran Van Duc, and Xuan Minh lay sprawled and torn in the dirt and mud, their bodies twisted and flailed, their reaching fingers within touching distance. They were a cell, and they had died as a cell, cut down by the first ragged burst from the machine gun that they knew had been silenced. The machine gun had come alive again, and that entire portion of the perimeter had stiffened with its punching and barking song. Only Minh, the last in line, had had time to form a thought as his screaming mouth dug into the dirt: *The leaders were wrong.* Other cells came behind, confident in the knowledge that the machine gun bunker and adjoining fighting holes had been taken out by the mortar barrage and lead cells. This is what they had been taught. They came, half-standing, leaning forward with their AK's, leaning forward into a decimating hail of machine-gun, rifle, and grenade fire. Those who were only wounded, or who lived a few seconds before dying, clearly heard the deep-throated animal cries of the American soldiers behind the guns—challenging cries taunting in their tone, reckless and wild and ferocious. The perimeter held. The three-man cell that carried two satchel charges and the flag of the PAVN crossed through the wire, into the storm, and was never seen again.

The smooth-faced lieutenant did not know the names of the three dead NVA soldiers he stepped over as he approached the large fighting hole. He knew one hundred and thirteen enemy dead had been counted in the wire and beyond so far. He had heard the resumption of machine-gun fire from this sector of the perimeter during the critical moments at the height of the attack, had recognized its importance, to gain strength from it to carry on, to get swept up in a surge of energy that marked the turning of the tide. From the moment the machine gun resumed its deadly tattoo, the Americans knew: they would hold.

The LT came to the hole. Sitting on the left edge was a new man from the engineer battalion, Diaz. He sat with his elbows on his knees, his face in his hands. His hands and what could be seen of his head were covered with specks of dried blood. His hair stood in spiky tufts. He did not look up at the LT.

On the right side of the hole was the big artilleryman, O'Meara. He leaned awkwardly against the side, his arms folded across his chest. His right hip and side were clumsily covered in bloody four-inch compresses. His right ear was torn and hanging by a thread of skin from his bloody skull, the hair matted and dirty. Three or four teeth shone whitely from the left corner of his lower mouth, where a quarter-sized chunk of lip was missing. His eyes shone wide and bright, watching as the LT looked at the third man.

The third man was the black soldier, Washington, an infantryman from the hill. Washington stood in the classic machine-gunner's stance, feet spread slightly, knees and hips against the front wall of the hole, shoulders rounded, right hand on the trigger grip, left over the feed cover. His right cheek was pressed against the stock, his eyes open and staring down the length of barrel toward the wire where the enemy lay. The eyes would stare into the wire forever. All around him were brass shell casings, testimony to his volume of fire through the night. Sprawled in front of the hole and in the wire were the remains of the cells, *dead* cells, testimony to

Washington's accuracy and determination. The LT had to kneel and look closely, but he found the wounds that had killed Washington: two high in his chest, one in the throat. The front of the man's jungle fatigue shirt was purple-syrupy, soaked with thick blood.

The LT knew the gun team had abandoned their M-60 after a rocket blew their bunker. He knew they had lost five KIA overall, fifteen or sixteen wounded. He knew the wounded assistant gunner had dragged the wounded gunner through the raging battle to the command bunker, where the assistant gunner had died while they cared for the gunner. Knew that he and the others in the command bunker had guessed the M-60 was at the least out of action, at the worst being turned against them by the NVA.

He looked now at the distance between the fighting hole he stood before and the M-60 bunker several yards away. He imagined crawling through the fire from the hole to the bunker, grabbing the gun, some ammo, and dragging it all back to the hole and setting it up. He imagined loading and firing the gun, knowing that without the gun the perimeter might be lost. He imagined leaning into the bucking gun, the hot shell casings *pinging, pinging, pinging* into the night, the tracers reaching out, the tracers reaching in. He imagined standing behind the gun and firing long after you *knew* you had been hit and were bleeding to death. *Why*, thought the lieutenant, *how?*

O'Meara, as if reading the LT's thoughts, as if hearing the question out loud, looked first at Diaz, then at Washington and his machine gun, and said carefully and quietly through his torn mouth, "It was his war, Lieutenant."

Breathe Deep

I SAT near the military crest of a mountain in the Central Highlands with my M-16 lying locked and loaded across my legs. My feet in their worn jungle boots dangled against the smooth rock I sat on. I faced west, watching the sun do its Oriental thing with the pastel purples, pinks, oranges, and reds as it began to set behind the far ranges toward Cambodia. My eyes followed the descent of my mountain as it swept gracefully into a forested valley, stepping down with triple and double canopy as it stumbled and nudged against a muddy river that snaked through the valley from my right to left. The six shades of green, confident in their hues in daylight, had already begun to flatten. They went into their nighttime combat look, browns to purples to gunmetal to silver, softened by shade, shadow, and mist . . . spilled and puddled liquids rather than mosaic.

It was a moment of natural quiet not violated by the pervasive sounds of war. No helicopter blades beat the air above the trees, no jet engines whistled above the clouds, no armored vehicles growled through the valley. There was no booming of artillery or tearing of machine-gun fire. There was not even the sound of quiet men at rest after a long, hot, uphill march through a jungle-forest alien and beautiful in the extreme. The platoon I was with had already slung their hammocks, dug their fighting holes, C-four'd their C-rats, checked their equipment, cursed their LT, the ARVN, Westmoreland, LBJ, the war, Jane, Uncle Ho, Charlie, and life, and had settled down with their own thoughts.

I was in the relaxed state heavy physical exertion will bring. I wasn't ready to fall asleep, but my muscles ached pleasantly, my blood throbbed, my sweat had dried, and my mouth found moisture again. I took myself away from the men of the platoon—most of them I did not know anyway—and found the rock near the crest of the mountain. I felt the warm deep hug of loneliness embrace me. It was a relatively new feeling for me as a young man, loneliness—or aloneness—but I was already on intimate terms with it. It came to me early in my time in Vietnam, deepened as the nights and experiences were gathered and devoured, and planted a seed that became deeply rooted in me for the rest of my life.

My thoughts drifted back to my first real night in-country, spent on the hill base camp at Pleiku. I was shown a cot in a small house made of sandbags. I was shown the latrine. I was shown a "fighting bunker," where I was to go if we were attacked. I was told I would get my assignment in the morning. I was given no weapon. I sniffed the rotten sandbags, I sniffed the latrine, the cooling night air, my emotions, and knew immediately there would be no sleep that night. At almost midnight some type of signal was given and men all around my sandbag house came awake and ran here and there holding their bouncing helmets in one hand, their M-14's or M-16's with the other. I had been watching the sporadic launching of flares, carefully studying the sweeping open countryside beyond the wire under their swaying and sputtering light, in an attempt to spot any enemy sappers who might be crawling through the wire toward my sandbag house. I heard hollow booms, close, and shouted orders. Two officers appeared and stood behind a sandbag wall in front of my house talking in low tones and watching the wire. I cleared my throat and stood next to them, not part of their conversation, not part of their unit, not part of their night. They both had weapons. I had my Buck "General" hunting knife my friend Dave had given me before we shipped over. I did not draw it from the sheath, but placed it on top of the sandbags and held it tight. I waited for the enemy all that night, knife in hand, heart in throat, and was rewarded with the dawn. But that had been many months, many nights ago. My thoughts came back to *this* night.

Being in a different place with different smells, sounds, values, tastes, workaday gear—a place clearly separated from the known, from home, from known smells, sounds, and things—this signposted the loneliness. Vietnam was not home, was nothing like *my* world, and any attempt by the military—hot meals, radio music, soft drinks—had an insidious reverse effect. But this constituted only the surface layer of loneliness. The depth and intensity came from the *life* lived there in that strange world, a life that required me to go about the business of death. I dressed for it, equipped myself for it, traveled, communicated, planned, and acted for it. War means death. We came to war; I was part of the daily business of war. The enemy was out there in that alien landscape, terrorizing, stealing, lying, booby-trapping, ambushing, attacking, warring against his *own* people to force his ideology on them. He was also out there, the skulking bastard, to try to kill *me*, and this I would not allow. Riding in a Huey as it descended into a hot LZ while clutching an M-16 5.56mm automatic assault rifle in my hands and a 50:1 grid map in my teeth, dressed in sweaty jungle fatigues draped with ammo and hand grenades, ready to leap off the chopper into a raging battle with zealous armed men determined to kill was a tilting departure from driving my '53 Chevy (white over butterscotch with baby moons, six in-line, three-on-the-tree) along A1A while listening to the Beach Boys on WQAM with ol' Rick Shaw the DJ, wearing cutoffs, surfer sandals, a clean white T-shirt, and dark shades, hip to hip with a long-legged long-haired long-lashed tanned and smooth girl wearing short shorts, a smile, and a flimsy top stretched over rising breasts that would know the warmth of my palms before the day was out. A departure.

Thinking about the girl, the car, the music, the life back home in the World will kick-start the mid-level lonelies. But to get in deep, *deep* in lonely, into an aloneness with medieval intensity, then you have to get to the night in Vietnam. I know there were nights along the coast and up against the DMZ. I know there were nights in Hue and Saigon, Dak To and Lang Vei, Da Nang, My Tho, Vung Tau, and the Delta. I know there were nights offshore, and at twenty thousand feet. My Vietnam nights came to me in the highlands.

Triple canopy in the highlands is cathedrallike, still, serene, and echoey. Often the trail underfoot is clear and hard, easy to walk, with moss-covered rock alongside it. Often the sun angles down through the reaching trees, softly textured by mist, smoke, and dust. If there has been rain it will patter, patter against the leaves until it splashes against your neck or face. If it is dry the leaves will rustle the branches above your head, scratch at your pant leg. Visibility can be many yards, as the scrub is often sparse. You can see down the trail, follow the ridge to your right or the slope to your left, you can see movement against the backdrop of greens. Or none.

The night does not dim the cathedral. Sure, it erases the majestic columns, the reaching branches, the umbrella gathering of leaves. It takes away the trail, the moss, the rocks. They are hidden from your eyes but you know you're still in the cathedral because the echoes, the misty smell, the awareness of distance and volume remain. Just as in the cathedral every footfall is shared, so it is in the triple canopy of the highlands. It forces a quiet time, that atmosphere. You do not want to go clanking and grunting along the center aisle between the pews, draped in your vestments of death, propelled by your desire to reach the altar. No. You wish to sit and reflect, gather your thoughts, give thanks for your breath, wrap yourself in quiet, open your senses to receive the Word, and wait. You wait for the footfall, the misstep, the fullness of shadow or form. With dry mouth and trembling fingers you let them approach, their collection plate a pith helmet, their chanted dogma perverse in its form and substance. Their stealthy feet tread across and upon the Word with arrogant ignorance, and when they finally, hesitantly, come into range of your ministry you bless them with a fire-and-brimstone sermon aimed at teaching them the folly of life and the certainty of death.

Now you begin to know the depth, real depth. Night brings it, night in Vietnam, night at war. Death stands beside life, leans against it, embraces it. You become aware of how achingly fine the line, how short the distance, how quick the time between breath and none, thought and none, dreams . . . and none.

After the unreal and elongated seconds following the fire that rips the night, after the explosions, the flares, the screams, the punching coughing ripping shards of hot metal,

after the cathedral becomes quiet again (each soul in attendance silent in introspection and self-evaluation) you reflect
on the truth of what you have heard and witnessed. Your
heart still pumps; blood throbs your temples. Your brain still
has thoughts, your body still has nerve ends, you feel your
hands sweat and your testicles relax. You still have needs: your
mouth thirsts for water, your ears thirst for sounds of peace.
You still have dreams, you still have life. You look to your left,
your right, your front. You see how close, how thin the line,
how ephemeral the wall between what you are and what *they*
are. They are dead. Without life. They have no dreams, no
thirst. They are merely twisted lumps of flesh already beginning to rot, impossibly still, slick-wet, discolored, shattered,
and burst. They are no longer what you are. But *you* are, ter-
rifyingly, wondrously.

I sat on the mountain that night cloaking myself in
thoughts of loneliness. Night had pushed away the six shades
of green, and the ridges and peaks of the highlands stretched
away before me somber and full. A hot moon hung over the
mists; beneath the mists lay the carpet of forest-jungle slop-
ing away, the vastness of it all pleasing to me. I breathed in
and out, in and out, seeing my breath—my life's breath—mix
into and join the blue mists that shrouded the valley and the
path across the river.

Each breath a loneliness. Each night of loneliness another
breath.

Slick

THE Huey was a cool machine.

Even when I boarded the Huey helicopter en route to a hot LZ, or an insertion into Indian country for a three-day hump through the boonies, or as part of a quick-response platoon being lifted into a position flanking some unit pinned down by ambush, I would get the rush. Riding in those choppers open to the wind was exhilarating, your legs dangling over the side above the skids, the six shades of green in quilted symmetry or humpbacked tumble waffling along beneath. The air was cooler, the smells filtered, the sights given a crisper photo-image look by height and distance. Often I was amazed at the sight of that thick, deep, richly green carpet of jungle-forest that stretched and rolled away to the west and north, miles and miles of wild untamed land inhabited by all kinds of exotic creatures. The Huey would lift me above it all, the villages, the roads, the jungle, the open valleys, the craggy climbing mountain ridges—lift me above it, put it on display, and make it mine to capture and hold.

Often when I flew in the choppers a popular tune rocked around in my skull. It was called "Fire"—not the Doors' "Light My Fire." It had a demonic-satanic sound for those days, and the singer became more shrill and agitated as the song progressed, ending by intoning the word "fire" over and over again. Maybe it was the rhythm of the blades, the beat of the blood in my temples, or the pulsing fear of the unknown as I flew into battle.

We, as mere human beings made of flesh, blood, thought, dreams, prayer, and spit, absorb power and energy from the machines we use. Flying in the choppers actually helped me pump myself up for what lay ahead. I was with some number of armed men, armed like me with grenades, M-16's, and radios. We dropped out of the sky into a harsh, hostile, forbidding, and immense landscape peopled by tenacious and determined soldiers armed and anxious to kill us. Many of us were teenagers, wide-eyed and dry-mouthed, very aware of our vulnerability and mortality. But as we descended we unconsciously drank from the well of power—the noise, the wind, the feeling of lift, the weight of steel and aluminum, the heat of turbine and sun on dark green paint, the forward momentum, the throaty chatter of door-gunner fire. It came to us, permeated our psyche, charged us with strength even as our teeth clenched and the knuckles on hands that gripped our M-16's went white.

We are comin' *down*. We are comin' down *into* it, comin' down to be part of this contact, this engagement, this extraction, this flanking movement, this battle, this *war*. Yeah . . . you, the *main force* VC or the *veteran* 320 NVA Battalion. Yeah . . . you in those bunkers, you with your AK's, RPG's,

and Chi-Coms. You layin' your fire into the American positions or those American grunts advancing on you across a
hot, wide-open, not-one-fucking-place-to-hide rice paddy.
Good, just hold on.

There was always an urgency about getting *off* the Huey as
it flared a couple of feet above the ground, like you were
aware—hot LZ or not—that you wanted to un-ass the chopper and let it get back into the sky where it belonged. You
would clamber out, trying to hold onto your equipment, hat,
maps, *gear* in the hurricane whirlwind created by the digging
blades, trying to move away from the chopper, find cover,
keep your weapons pointed toward where the enemy might
be, and stay alive. You did this in a rush of power you si-
phoned off during the ride in.

With this came an almost palpable diminishment, a reduc-
tion in the surrounding envelope of intensity, as the roar and
thud of the lifting chopper cleared the ground and waffled
away from your back, which was already feeling the heat of
the sun across it. Your face had been cut by the edge of the tall
grass, your boots had scuffed and stumbled through clods of
dirt or puddles of human waste in the paddies, and now sound
came back—sound without the chopper. Even if it was the
sound of a raging firefight it was still less full after the Huey
made its drop and leaned forward to climb away. I was acutely
aware of it the first time and every time it happened, but
quickly learned I could shrug it off—the feeling of being
somehow weakened, I mean. I could retain the power and energy given me by that wondrous and capable machine, and
lean into whatever waited for me on the ground.

It has been said that war can be a powerful and moving
spectacle. To see a battalion-size lift—three long rows of
Hueys in line on the field or runway, squads of combat-
equipped soldiers shuffling out and climbing aboard, the long

line shuddering, rocking, then leaning forward nose-down in the classic Huey liftoff as it gained speed and momentum and clattered into the waiting sky—it *was* moving. On big lifts and small I have sat on the floor edge with my boots dangling over the skids, bumping and bouncing through the cool blue, watching a lovely, chunky, workhorse faded-green chopper just like mine flying alongside a few yards away. Sometimes it looked as if their rotor-blade tips would touch and you could clearly see the features on the faces of the pilots and others on board. Off in the distance the gunships would circle their flock. Often the LZ was prepped by fire, the gunships waiting for a reaction from the enemy, ready to strike.

A crew chief or door gunner would signal when we got close enough to the LZ to begin our descent, and our mouths would go dry. Below, we could see the smoke, dust, explosions, and fire of battle, gunships and fast-movers making their runs, clumps of artillery bursting in the tree lines, orange and green tracers crisscrossing insanely through a clearing. Your mind could not resist the inevitable "Oh, man . . . this is *it*," and then came the leaning circling who-dropped-the-bottom-out-of-the-ride swoop, then the flare, someone shouting (it may have been *you*), "*Go, go* . . . get *out* . . . Move, move, *move* . . ."

Much has been written about the men who flew the medevacs, the "dustoffs." There are not enough words. They came for us when we were wounded, hurt, and dying. They came for us when it was insane to do so, sometimes. They came for us, and they got us out of there.

During the last ride I had in a Huey I lay flat on my back on a stretcher, naked except for my dogtags. I clutched my Buck hunting knife against my chest under the clean white sheet someone had thrown over me. The Huey lifted off into the wet cold air of central Japan, taking me to the hospital at

Camp Zama. My stretcher was on the floor. Sitting in the jump seats were two young Navy officers; maybe they were doctors. The one with glasses looked at me a moment, shrugged out of his khaki jacket, leaned forward, and draped it over me. I was immediately warmer, and soon fell asleep.

Thank you, sir.

The Huey was a cool machine.
I rode it through six shades of green.

Napalm

ANGER has remained deeply embedded in me for over thirty years, an integral part of the whole entity, a core sustaining the lesser emotions.

It is a recognized reality, my anger, recognized but not clearly defined or identified. It is a continuous pulsing energy thrumming through the soles of my feet as they tread the deckplates of my psyche, like a powerful generator below the waterline.

Occasionally my anger is destructive, leaving broken things in its wake, tendrils of guilt and loss hanging from my sharp edges like flare parachutes fluttering from a burnt tree.

Mostly anger is the blood that flows through my veins, the air I breathe, my thoughts, dreams, memories. When I run in the heat I chew on it to make spit.

Anger drinks with me when I sip the Irish. It shoulders up to the bar, shoves sadness aside without breaking a sweat, looks around in disdain at all the virgin eyes, and asks in a voice laced with threat and anticipation, "What the fuck are *you* looking at?"

Extraction

My three-man team spent the night at one of the "Ivy League's" battalion HQ's. We had finished one operation with a Special Forces outfit and were on our way to another assignment. We had our own twelve hours or so of stand-down, to rest, recupe, suck down a Mr. Pibb's. We did not know anyone there, had no desire to socialize, and were happy to have a few moments to ourselves. I became antsy, though, and left my Recon and RTO sprawled with our gear. I sauntered over to the battalion tactical operation center because I was nosey and wanted to see if anything was going on.

The TOC was filled with majors, captains, several denominations of lieutenants, and a portly colonel who apparently figured if his haircut was masculine and warlike it would drag the rest of him with it. Everyone in there had tense faces, and they all bent in the direction of a bank of radios along one wall. Several EM's and noncoms bustled about also, but the words coming from the ether were the focus.

It was close to midnight, and somewhere to the west in the

trackless, ridged and ravined, scrubby and double-canopied jungle, a seven-man LRRP team was calling for help. The long-range patrols relied on stealth and camouflage to allow them to quietly observe the VC and NVA as they moved through different areas of operation. They carried light infantry firepower and could call for artillery or air support if needed (ideally), but spent most of their time attempting to *avoid* contact with the enemy. They were supposed to observe, call in intelligence or fire missions, and move to another location for more of the same. If by chance they were spotted by the enemy they would fight only to E&E—escape and evade. They were too small a unit to stand and fight against maneuvering platoons or companies, so they didi'd.

They did not panic when forced to evade or escape. They were all volunteers, trained, equipped, motivated, and tough. Most HQ's had special warehouses where the LRRP teams stored their balls, as they were way too big to carry around. They always went in with prearranged locations for extraction, then fallbacks if they missed the first or second. They would try to break contact, then run like hell for the extraction point so a chopper could swoop in and get their asses out of there.

Did I say chopper? That was why all the faces in the TOC were so tense that night. The LRRP team leader was grunting into the radio as he ran; saying he had two wounded, they were crashing and tumbling through the brush to the second fallback, and the NVA were within hearing distance behind them. He wanted to know the chopper would be ready to come in when they got to the extraction point because they would have only a small window of time before the NVA came in shooting. Problem was, there was no chopper. It wasn't the weather. The night had soft breezes, a few low-hanging clouds scattered around, and plenty of stars. It would be an easy flight for any experienced and ballsy pilot. I stood in a corner listening: the problem was that that evening, for some reason, all the choppers were either on loan to the ARVN, or over on the coast working with Division on a dawn cordon-and-search mission, or down for maintenance. Right then, right there, the battalion HQ could not find a chopper they could send out to snatch the LRRP team.

"Tell them again we're working on a chopper for them," said the colonel to the sergeant working the radio. The sergeant spoke into the handset in low tones.

"Did you say on the way? Confirm bird on the way?" responded the LRRP team leader.

"Tell him we're working on it," said the colonel briskly. "Tell him we're doing our best. Tell him to keep moving, to . . . stay in cover . . . to *evade*. Tell him we'll get him a chopper as soon as we can."

The sergeant murmured into the handset again, and the reply burst out of the radio and ricocheted around the TOC: "Now, *now*. We got two wounded. They're on our *ass*. We need a bird now. . . ."

I looked around the TOC at the radio operators, who were listening with one ear as they called other units trying to find a helicopter. I looked at the tense pale faces, at the beads of sweat on the colonel's round forehead. I stared at the radio, waiting again for the voice of the LRRP team leader, but there was nothing. Might be dead. Might be shot to pieces. Might be a prisoner of war. Might be shot to pieces *and* a prisoner of war. Might have simply gone to ground, hiding, lying burrowed into the foliage, chest heaving, hands clamped against the wounded men's mouths to stifle their groans. Hiding, waiting, and counting the stolen breaths until the dawn.

"Try them again," the colonel ordered the sergeant in an irritated voice. "Why don't they answer?"

I turned and walked out of the TOC.

I stood under the crystalline midnight sky, tried to stretch the tense kinks out of my muscles, and let the possible scenarios for the LRRP team play themselves out in my mind. Somewhere above me I heard the sound of a Huey circling the battalion HQ, and accepted it as part of the night sounds. Then it kicked into my brain. A *chopper*. They must have found one—but what the hell was it doing circling *here* when it should be hauling ass out to *there*?

The answer came to me in the blaring voice of a taped message booming down onto the ears of those in the camp through a large set of speakers mounted between the skids of the Huey.

"BUY U.S. SAVINGS BONDS. THE FOURTH IN-FANTRY DIVISION EXPECTS EVERY SOLDIER TO DO HIS PART BY BUYING U.S. SAVINGS BONDS. THIS IS A DIVISION DRIVE, MEN . . . SO LET'S ALL DO OUR PART. BUY U.S. SAVINGS BONDS."

The message was repeated as the chopper circled overhead twice, then faded as the bird clattered away to saturate other populated areas of the camp. I trudged back to my Recon and RTO, hands deep in my pockets, a frown on my face, my old friend anger clawing my ribs like a prisoner on Death Row clinging to his bars.

Eunuch's Rules

WAR is murder.

No matter what kind of word games you want to play, what kind of justification you apply, it will always return to the same simple act. Some person with weapons kills another person. The person killed may be armed, or not, may be actively engaged in an attempt to kill the other or actively fleeing, may be part of the support for the frontline soldiers or just living in the wrong place at the wrong time . . . it doesn't matter.

Being soldiers from a country built on moral and religious blueprints, we always go off to war with *rules*. We create the rules to intellectually lift ourselves above the murderous-animal level. We are taught to respect and adhere to the rules, and we punish those of us who don't. The most well-known set of war rules (war rules?) is the Geneva Convention. As U.S. soldiers we were actually issued a laminated card printed with these rules, along with a Military Code of Conduct card instructing us on how we should behave. We were given classes on all of this, of course, tested, drilled, and expected to keep it in the front of our mind at all times. Then we were issued the latest weaponry and sent out to find people and kill them.

If all the peoples of the world believed in words like "chivalry," "honor," "responsibility," and "justice," as we do, this would be swell. They don't. In fact, in many places they see any thoughts like these applied to the reality of war as a fatal weakness.

A cynically realistic observer from the North might say, "You came here to the jungle to fight a war against people who have a social, spiritual, and moral structure totally alien to yours, a people who have been at war with *someone* for over a thousand years, and you equipped your young soldiers with weapons *and* rules? Well, get that surprised look off your face."

I guess where I'm going with this is the fact that no matter what, many of us who fought in Vietnam went there, fought there, and came home from there with a sense of *not being totally wrong*. We recognized (even after only a few days in-country) war for what it is. We saw the horrific reality and result of our actions. We participated in the killing, sometimes in what could be perceived as self-defense, often as the aggressor. There was nothing nice about what we did, and many young Americans returned home from Vietnam carrying a lifetime of emotional and moral baggage because they could not fit what they did there into the good-guy, white-hat, American-hero skin they wore.

Fine. But many of us also realized the fact that the war *we* fought was different from the war *they* fought. Both sides used almost every weapon of war in their arsenal (their arsenal was supplemented enthusiastically by China *and* the Eastern Bloc heroes). They skipped across international boundaries to move men and materiel; we mined their harbor. We had our vaunted airpower, but did our best to blunt its effectiveness through the pervasive application of those wondrous *rules* (take a ride through Colonel Jack Broughton's *Thud Ridge* and *Going Downtown* for a taste of this). Both sides used ambush. Both sides had POW's (take a low crawl through the way *they* treated POW's, and the way *we* did). Both sides had their My Lais—ours were rare and highly publicized, theirs were continuous throughout the war and after and largely dismissed, ignored, defended, or rationalized by brave intellectuals.

This brings us to the ever popular mines and booby traps.

We most often used mines as a means of defense, as when a mine field was created around an observation post, a firebase, or a unit compound. The mines were sown to keep the enemy from reaching the inner wire or to channel him into selected firepower routes. The NVA, and especially the VC, used mines *offensively*. They would be deployed along a trail or likely approach to a village or tree line, and when a U.S. soldier or Marine set one off it meant dead or wounded, a halted movement, medevac helicopters, and time. Mined roadways interdicted supply routes, mined clearings refused possible LZ's. Often American units would lose a couple of guys to a mine out in the middle of *nowhere*. The mine maimed and killed, but it did not in any way alter the immediate military situation. It was just *there*, waiting for someone to come along and step on it.

And now we come to it, the booby trap. I wished then and I wish now I could sit and watch as a couple of VC or NVA "soldiers" sat on their haunches laughing and talking while they set up any one of the multitude of booby traps. Did they whistle under their breath? Did they look at their buddies' work and nod approvingly? Did they think they were winning the war with their cowardly and savage little tools of the devil? Sit there dipping burned and sharpened bamboo stakes into their own shit so when the stake cut its way into a soldier's foot the nasty puncture wound became an immediate site of infection? Carefully place a grenade at crotch level so when the tripwire is pulled the recipient takes the blast in his lower belly and groin? Then *leave*? Scurry away laughing. Off you go then, on to the next project. . . . You're not even in the area when the horror you've sown reaps its grisly and mindless reward of blood, tissue, and agony.

Why did I wish I could sit and watch them place their booby traps? Because I wanted to see if they looked like soldiers. You know, like an NVA or VC soldier with a pack, a pith helmet, Ho Chi Minh racing slicks, and an AK. Did they look like me, like a man? I wore a uniform, carried a flag, carried my weapon at the ready looking for a fight and ready to fight hard if one developed, and I walked into the jungles of Vietnam with my balls hanging and clanging, right there between my legs, no question. I always wanted to see if those booby-trap VC and NVA even *had* balls, or if what was hanging in a toadskin sack between their legs were actually two gangrenous eyeballs the size of Uncle Ho's. And instead of hanging there if they weren't actually pulled tight and tucked up inside their puckered assholes.

If during my time in combat I managed to kill any of those creatures masquerading as VC or NVA soldiers, I am pleased. If possible I would like to kill them again, perhaps once a week for the rest of my life, those sorry, cowardly eunuchs.

Earth Angel

"I WONDER if we'll see her tonight," said the machine-gunner.

My team was set to go out to a night ambush position with a light platoon from one of the American divisions in the highlands. We were deep in the forest-jungle west and north of Pleiku; there had been plenty of enemy movement and some contact during the week, and the chances were good we would see some action. Men go through the pregame jitters in various ways, and the time before saddle-up always churned the guts and dried the mouth. Sometimes there was horseplay, sometimes a noncom or LT would express his nervousness with a harsh inspection of the men's equipment, sometimes the men would simply sit in small groups or alone, their stomachs on the edge of nausea, their thoughts private. Sometimes they talked quietly of home or dreams, and once in a while, as on this evening, they told tales and revisited popular legends. There was almost a half-hour before it got dark enough to quietly leave the perimeter and amble downslope into the tree line from the company position. There was a slight breeze, high cloud cover, and no moon. The night would be dark and long, a very real suspension of comfort, the sunrise a distant dream.

"Now here he goes again," said the platoon sergeant with a grin toward the machine-gunner. "Man's obsessed with this crazy story about the blonde in the bush."

"Yeah, but did she have a blond bush?" asked a reclining grunt, his voice muffled by the helmet covering his face.

The machine-gunner, a big shaggy man with thick glasses—we had already learned he was "seriously smart," and he always humped well-thumbed paperback books with him into the boonies—was inevitably nicknamed Professor. He shrugged. "Mock me, unbelievers, continue your dreary lives clothed in ignorance and boredom. The story has too valid and tenacious a history to be without substance. Not only has it been passed on by word of mouth around countless campfires, it has also been documented and honored by the all-powerful written word."

"Oooh, you mean you can find it in *books*, Professor?"

"You, sad idiot, will never find it in a book, that much we know for sure. That is why *I* feel compelled to present it verbally for your edification and enlightenment."

My RTO, Recon, and I had only worked with these guys a few days, but I was comfortable enough to venture, "Okay. You have our attention. *Who her?*"

"Ah, Lieutenant," replied the machine-gunner, "I knew you were a discerning personage in spite of your being a commissioned officer. The who-her you're asking about is the blonde observed on patrol with the Viet Minh forces back during the other debacle of a war here in this wondrous Vietnam."

"Blonde . . . as in *girl?*" I prodded.

"Girl indeed," responded the machine-gunner, "the nubile and pneumatic kind. One of those creatures with the smooth skin, soft red lips, pouty breasts with arrogant strawberry nipples, silky inner thighs leading to that incredibly wondrous place that accounts for every breath we and every man who has ever held his own erect phallus in his lonely hand has ever taken, every dream . . . every . . ."

"He means pussy," the helmet said.

"We have the picture, okay?" I said. "Don't torment us, just tell the damn story."

The big machine-gunner shook his head sadly, sniffed, and said, "Your impatience, Lieutenant, is illustrative of your lack of understanding and appreciation of such a complex and multitextured subject."

"Will you get *on* with it, Professor?" grumbled the sergeant. He sat a few feet away with his back against a tree, his M-16 balanced across his knees. "I'm already losing the hard-on I had hearing about the arrogant nipples."

"There was a night patrol set in ambush, much like ours will be this night," began the machine-gunner. "They were French troops, tough, proud, brave, marginally equipped and deplorably led. They were deep in the bowels of the triple canopy—perhaps we should say the very *womb* of this green world. They waited as we will, with their balls shriveled to the size of raisins, their mouths so dry their tongues felt like salt-covered leeches writhing across their lips, their eyes straining to catch a glimpse of the ghostlike jungle fighters who were the fathers of *our* ghostlike jungle fighters, their ears starving for that first betraying sound—"

"Fuckin' *forget* the hard-on *I* had."

The machine-gunner paused, cast a disapproving glance

at the sergeant, and carried on. "Finally they came. The enemy. A Viet Minh patrol mincing in their very Oriental and menacing way through the gloom. And with them—"

"Finally we get to the pussy—"

"—with them was the blonde."

After a quiet moment crowded with pulsating thoughts, I commanded, "Tell us."

"They say she was petite, but *ripe*. Female all the way," offered our storyteller. "And you know the French when it comes to *this* kind of observation. We can trust they knew what they were talking about when they said she wore green fatigues—wore them well, like a soldier. She wore no hat, allowing her golden hair to shine nicely in the green shadows, and she moved with a fluid ease and confidence with the other soldiers. They say her face was not plain by any means, pretty, lovely . . . beautiful perhaps. Pursed lips, brow creased in concentration, eyes bright and alive and searching the trail ahead of her. There has been passed down through the years a discrepancy. Often one will hear she carried a weapon, the old M-1 carbine, then one will hear she only carried some type of leather folder, or notebook. Was she a soldier? A journalist? A freelancer in pursuit of some *truth*? We don't know. We *do* know she wasn't a prisoner or camp follower, a comfort girl forced along for the pleasure of the troops. No. Our witnesses tell us she was too confident, too soldierlike, too self-possessed to simply be a sex object for the Viet Minh."

"We could *use* some comfort girls in this man's army," opined the sergeant.

"Sheeit, yeah," agreed another soldier lying in the crushed grass nearby. "I been beatin' my meat so much over here 'cause I can't get no pussy, if I ever *do* get laid again I'll have to keep my right hand behind my back so it don't get jealous."

The machine-gunner, used to being interrupted, nodded sagely and said in a kind voice, "A common lament, young troop, a common lament."

"And that's *it*?" I asked, wanting more. "That's the story?"

"Yeah," said my RTO, speaking up for the first time from the other side of my ruck, "did they waste 'em in the ambush? Did they kill them *and* her? Did they capture her, take her back to their camp, and introduce her to Colonel Lingus and his napalm tongue?"

"Goodness," said a genuinely shocked Professor, "you sound as if you should *immerse* yourself in the fleshpots of Kuala Lumpur, young radio soldier."

"He just got back," I said.

The machine-gunner shook his head, took off his glasses and fiddled with them, took a deep breath, and went on. "No, LT . . . that is not *it*. Legend has it that our Frenchmen in ambush were so taken aback by the presence of the blonde in such an incongruous setting they simply watched her until she, and the accompanying Viet Minh, were swallowed up by the gloom. Forever gone, but forever captured in legend."

"But there *is* more, right, Professor?" asked the muffled voice.

"Yes, dammit, there is more," agreed the machine-gunner. We waited.

"The French soldiers and the Viet Minh are ancient history in this tortured land," our storyteller began again, "so the legend of the blonde seems very far removed from our reality. This has been corrected by a new and current legend—"

"One of our Lurp teams," I suggested quietly.

"Yes, LT, one of our brave and mysterious Lurp teams. I have heard that *their* patrol took place very near where we are tonight, here in the forest of the highlands, deep and warm and green. Sharp-eyed observers they are, those long-range-patrol troopers. Of course they are, they work in a constant state of intense terror. . . . No matter. Story is, one of our Lurp teams lay in wait one night for the vaunted VC or heroic NVA soldiers to make their appearance on the moonlit trail, and when they did they had with them . . . the blonde."

"Same blonde?"

"Man, I hope not—"

"Hell, yeah, if she's the same one she's got some *miles* on her jungle ass—"

"Shit, by now *her* ass would look like *your* ass."

"What you talkin' about? Last night I saw how you was scopin' my cheeks and lickin' your lips."

"Well, if you'd quit wearing that lipstick and the lace undies on patrol—"

"Gentlemen. Gentlemen," admonished the machine-gunner with one raised palm. "No need to reveal our varied sexual proclivities for the visiting LT, right?"

It was quiet for a moment. Someone made a kissing sound. Someone said, "Fuck you." Someone said, "Best piece of ass you'll ever have."

Finally I had to ask, "And this *new* story with our Lurp team. How does *it* end?"

"They described the young lady in similar fashion," responded the machine gunner. "Yes, I said 'young lady' . . . for she is young. She is *not* the same woman seen by the Frenchmen." He nodded twice, as if this was very important to him. Then he continued, "She wore contemporary jungle fatigues, she may or may not have carried a weapon, she was comfortable on the trail, and she was absolutely beautiful and totally female—"

"Wonder if they could *smell* her? You know, that girl smell, like when you're slow-dancing and you put your face down against her hair and breathe it in?"

The reverie began.

"Man . . . maybe we'll see her tonight—"

"We got to figure a way to waste the dinks without hurting *her*. Then we'll pull her off the trail, she'll see we are the good guys, and she'll want to somehow *thank* us . . . you know—"

"What, a kiss on both cheeks like the doughnut-dollies give out?"

"No, man. *Really* thank us."

"Like go behind the bushes with every grunt in this sorry outfit? You crazy?"

The machine-gunner's raised palm again brought them to a halt. "Gentlemen," he began, "all of you have entirely missed the essence of detail in my narration."

We waited.

"If, perchance," he said with a smile, "the young lady chose to behave in the manner of your fantasy, it is clear she would derive her arousal and eventual satisfaction from being in the company of a soldier physically strong enough to carry the platoon's machine gun and at the same time worldly and intellectual enough to intrigue and stimulate her imagination as well as her libido."

"What did he say?"

"Something about her labia—"

"I wonder if she really *is* out there," someone said to the night, and we became quiet again.

The blonde came to all of us that night as we lay motionless and silent, the warm green gloom wrapped around us like a comforter, a ten-yard section of the trail barely visible in the night shadows. While we lay in ambush our minds reviewed the legend, held it up to the light, turned it over and around, softly stroked it, created hypothetical scenarios. She made love with each of us during the hours, in her own way. Then, smiling, she left us to stand awkward and shyly grinning at other images.

For me the vision was a sixteen-year-old velvet wisp of a girl from central California. She, too, had blond hair, but hers was long and silky, parted in the middle, shiny and light. She came from the San Joaquin farm country, with a caramel tan over unblemished skin. She had gray eyes broken into inquisitive prisms, a straight nose, and a small mouth with soft lips she nibbled with gently as she kissed me. She was a child-woman, to be sure, with small breasts easily cupped into the palms of my hands, and firm button nipples. When my fingers slid below her navel and found the essence of her it was warm-wet and pulsing, very small beneath a smudge of dark gold down. She waited until the deep misty hours to come up the trail alone. She stopped, naked and golden, her bare feet wet and muddy, leaned forward from the waist, and said quietly, "I still don't understand. Tell me again why you have to go." I didn't know what to say, and after a moment she shrugged, turned, and walked silently into the green.

A few moments or hours later, *they* came. A combination of fatigue, fear, stress, the night, and the intensity of my imagination and memory gave me a bad few seconds as I struggled to come to grips with their arrival. It was *them*, a fucking NVA squad, and this was *now*, and their point man suddenly stiffened, crouched, and threw his arm back in warning, and our ambush was sprung with a hellish and sustained roar made of automatic rifle and machine-gun fire, grenades, claymores, and hoarse screams.

We had placed your basic L-shaped ambush, and they had walked right in. Hard to say if they all made it to the kill zone before their point finally sensed it, but they had fire in their faces, fire from their left, and if they sought cover to their right they entered the claymore patterns. The silence that followed the thundering firefight was hollow and echoing, as if a large dome had been placed over that piece of the jungle. The screams died to moans, then silence. Rustling and rattling could be heard now and then as our medic crawled around caring for our wounded, and as their survivors tried to crawl away. Theirs was the more furtive sound, and drew immediate bursts of fire. To still be alive was to breathe deeply the sweet wet air, to admire the shape and height of the surrounding trees, to take comfort in the embracing earth.

Dawn came in a tumble as the gloom turned gray, then silver, then faded to let in the first metallic greens. We were able to make a cautious recon and assessment, a soft-step down the trail, mouths open, fingers on the triggers. Found five of them dead, twisted and sprawled. Their one wounded was the lame point. He had leapt away from the fire and into the claymore blast. He half-sat in a small hollow scooped out in the dirt under some shrub, holding his intestines in his hands and forearms, looking up at us and sobbing quietly. We stared at him for a few seconds, then someone gave him a burst of three that spun his pleading eyes away from us. Six enemy KIA.

We had two wounded, both able to walk out. We prepared to saddle up.

"Maybe she was with their *second* squad," said one of the grunts.

"No, man . . . She was on the tail of this one, but we sprung it too soon. We sprung it too soon."

"How you say that? We was all lookin', nobody saw her, nobody saw her turn and run. We were lookin', we woulda *seen* her—"

"She was probably with their *second* squad—"

"Knock off the bullshit," said the sergeant with a soft intensity. "Will you assholes *forget* the blonde for now? We still got to hump it back to the perimeter, and in case you shitbirds already forgot, we got *hit* the last time we returned from a night pos."

"Maybe it was *her,* the last time. She scoped us during the night, then—"

"Oh, for chrissakes . . ."

We stepped into the green, paralleling the trail but not on it. There was a momentary bunching as the grunts settled into their separation, and I saw the big machine-gunner turn as he adjusted the sling on his M-60. He pushed his glasses up on his nose, shrugged, and said quietly, "Maybe we'll see her tomorrow."

Listen

CHOPPERED in with three SF berets and a light platoon of their Montagnards. Un-assed the Huey and hurried into the shade. Looked like parts of Texas where they put us in: dry grass, big boulders, felled trees. Open rolling areas behind us as we turned our backs, tilted our faces up. Within seconds we were swallowed by the green carpet that ridges and rumps its way up the jagged hills-to-mountains. Within an hour we left the dry behind, left the scrub, and entered the rich loamy cathedral of forest-jungle highlands.

My team of three walked behind the SF LT. One of his sergeants was with the leading Yards, one with the trailing. Except for low guttural commands there is no talk. Controlled breathing, the tongue's silent inspection of dried lips. The Yards are good soldiers. They are solid men of short stature, mahogany-skinned, with aboriginal faces and gnarled hands. Their weapons and gear were well-maintained; they carried themselves with ease and confidence in the jungle, and they were loyal to Americans, especially the SF types. As

we step-listen-breathed, a continuous moving pause, or paus-
ing move, I saw that half of them carried their weapons at the
ready to the right, the others to the left. The SF LT told us in
the chopper the Yard who would walk point was a veteran soldier and a mystic. They deployed flank teams on either side.
It would be difficult to surprise us in ambush.

The hours wore on, and we climbed. We took a couple of
kneeling breaks, sucked on our canteens, munched candy.
Then, up. The Beret LT had told us during the briefing our
mission was to look for new VC/NVA supply routes coming
in from Cambodia. Aggressive patrols and ambushes from
the SF camps, and heavy insertions and sweeps by U.S. infantry units, had compromised many of the known VC supply
trails. The gooks were getting blown off their bicycles at an
alarming rate, captured documents lamented, so they were
looking for other avenues of approach. Now we would look,
too. Our mission was one of recon, but if a fight developed,
we'd fight. That was why the usually self-reliant SF had asked
for my little team. I was the two-niner, the shavetail with a radio and an attitude. If we got hit the Yards would pull back
into a tough little perimeter, the SF lieutenant would give me
the nod, and I'd call in the shit on Charlie's gook ass. (That's
how I talked. Your utterances had to complement and be representative of your capabilities.)

Step, pause, look, breathe. Step, pause, look, breathe. As
we climbed higher into the mountains the terrain grew truly
spectacular. We got into the sweeping stands of giant hardwoods, spongy-carpeted and open beneath them, the green
umbrella canopy far above our heads almost unbroken.
Where there was an opening in the trees, the clear blue sky
could be glimpsed far beyond, the light filtering in almost flu-
orescent. A signal would come like a silent arrow from one of
the flank teams, and we would all sink to an expectant crouch,

weapons ready, trigger fingers vibrating in anticipation. Once or twice when this happened I found myself shouldered up against one of the reaching giants, my dry mouth open, my straining eyes trying to warp corners around the huge rocks and other trees. When no enemy came, when the suspension of time wasn't torn by a ripping burst of machine-gun fire or *crunch-thud* of grenades, I'd take a breath. Then I looked at the tree, the girth, thickness, the height of bare column trunk before the first thick branches arched out. Some trunks were smooth, others might have a rough gray bark, or a wrinkled brown skin invaded by black and purple veinlike vines. During the immeasurable seconds of waiting for ambush those trees embraced me, stood strong for me, provided me with shelter. Then another signal, the stand and stretch, the hitch and pull at gear, and the step, pause, look, breathe continued.

We stepped across brooks with cold clear water tumbling melodically over shiny-smooth brown, black, and gray rocks. We climbed boulders, each passing his weapon to the man above him as we swung up and onto felled giants lying from one end of our vision to the other in the foliage. Then down the other side, easy-does-it along the mossy rocks, and on. Once we came to a beautiful mountain pond at the base of a hundred-foot waterfall. The boulders were black-wet and slick, the veil of misting water cool as it fell against our cheeks. We climbed an almost sheer rock wall on the opposite side of the falls, and at the top took a break.

Behind us descended the trail we had climbed. To our right ran the small stream that became the waterfall and pond below. To our left, the hardwood giants continued their climb. Now, slung wide and open before us, a sweeping valley rolled away in tumbled green confusion at our feet. Have I used the word "spectacular" already? It was.

We rested, talking quietly, and I doubt I was the only one

who wondered what it would be like to someday shoulder a ruck, whistle for a chesty yellow Lab, grab a good walking stick, and hike out into that incredible country when there was no war.

But there was a war, and we were in it. We left the clearing behind and went back into the jungle, back to the step, pause, look, breathe. *They* were out there somewhere, hiking through the landscape, their AK's at the ready, their eyes searching, searching. Maybe they were as taken by the beauty of the landscape as I was, or maybe for them it was just there. I don't know. I do know we would try very hard to kill each other if our paths crossed, and I would not hesitate for one second to call in enough explosive steel to reduce that entire Walden-like haven to gravel and sawdust.

We came finally to our night pos, and quietly set in. The perimeter was placed and tied by the SF sergeants, the LT checked in on his net and I called in preset fire coordinates on mine. We ate CIDG-rats (civilian indigenous rations), smelled the tangy sauce the Yards used, and talked in low tones for a few minutes. Then we settled in for the night. Darkness came like a blanket at first; then my eyes gradually adjusted and I was able to see here and there through the canopy. Brittle stars hung and winked. At ground level the bulges and shapes took their places, the shadows took their textures, and the black woolly terrain shrugged into its nightclothes and squatted there in front of me.

The night was interrupted only by my imagination. Three or four times I came suddenly awake for no reason. When that happened I let my senses appraise the immediate situation, discover no threat, and tell me to relax. I would remain awake for a few moments, experiencing the black, then fall asleep again, one hand on my M-16. Came the morning. Stinging black coffee superheated over a sunspot of C-4, a bad case of jungle bed-head (there is no bed-head like *jungle* bed-head), and stiff joints. Strange morning smells coming from the Yards, a lengthy and minutely intricate display of personal hygiene performed by one of the SF sergeants, and we were on our feet and off.

Did they stretch and groan as they reached for their AK's and balls of rice? Did they long for a current copy of the *Hanoi Bugle* when they squatted behind a bush with their pants down around their ankles? Did they wish they could just go home and forget the whole thing? I don't know. I *do* know they were out there, and *we* were out there, and the SF lieutenant stayed serious most of the time, and one of his sergeants had fresh minty breath, and the Yards seemed to grin a lot and carried their grenades by threading the pull-pin through the pocket buttonholes on their fatigues, and it seemed like a long time since I had heard the sound of a helicopter overhead, and my feet itched and I wished I could go back and bathe in that waterfall, and I wondered if there was some way to contact General Giap and suggest to him that this mountain area was more suited to spiritual enlightenment and renewal than to resupply routes.

We did the dry-mouthed eyeball-straining step, pause, look, breathe for two more days and nights before being lifted out and choppered back to the SF camp.

It was very beautiful, and real.

They were still out there, part of the landscape like a tick on a fawn.

Snapshot

I DID not receive the classic "Dear John" letter while I was in Vietnam, but I did have one hell of a week right in the middle of my tour. The always efficient U.S. Mail hunted me down while my team was attached to the 3rd ARVN Armored on Highway 14 between Pleiku and Dak To. I got three letters from the World, three different days; two included photos.

The first letter was from my father, who wrote on behalf of my youngest brother. My old man assured me that my brother felt "real bad" about the situation, but at least no one had gotten hurt. My brother did indeed look dejected in the photos, which illustrated with flashbulb clarity how my nice shiny Opel Kadet, deep blue with wide white racing stripes, looked after being rolled over into a ditch alongside State Road 84. It was totally crunched, and my old man included the information that my brother felt the accident "wasn't his fault entirely."

The second letter was from my mom. She and my first

serious girlfriend had become friends through the years. My first girl had told me straight out she had no intention of waiting for me while I went off to war, and sure enough she went ahead and got married to a rather swarthy fellow with lots of oil in his hair. How did I know what he looked like? My mom went to their wedding, took lots of snapshots, and sent them to me so I'd know what a swell time everyone had.

Finally came the letter from California. There were no photos, and it wasn't from the girl I had left behind. It was from *her* mom. She and I had developed a close and good re-lationship while I spent time with her daughter, and she felt I should know that the girl I called mine was not only seeing another guy, he was an ex–*Air Force* type, and they were to be wed shortly. Ooooh-kay.

That evening the South Vietnamese soldiers I was with (and possibly a few *North* Vietnamese troops too) were puz-zled and entertained by their young American forward ob-server LT, who climbed to the top of the largest bunker in the compound, tore what appeared to be a fistful of letters and photos into pieces, flung them into the wind toward the far jungle, and shouted, "Enough already! Go ahead and *shoot* me for cryin' out loud!"

Secondaries

"**C**APRICIOUS" is a genteel and playful word, a word you would not think has a place in an exploration of war. But war has a capricious nature sometimes—capricious, mystifying, and deadly. Things happen that make a mockery of reason, if *any* reason can be associated with the business of war.

Lieutenant David Palanzi is in a shallow hole during a firefight, calling in artillery fire as the forward observer and acting as grunt platoon leader at the same time. They are involved in a nasty little affair, and the tracers are crisscrossing, mortars are falling, and grenades are being lobbed back and forth. Dave has gone to great lengths and some expense to have his jungle fatigues tailored to fit him tightly; no baggy green pants for this guy. He is tough, he is respected by the troops, and he intends to *look good* while out and about. Suddenly during the mêlée he sees a Chi-Com grenade come wobbling out of the smoke and dust and land a couple of feet behind him. His eyes see it, and his mind instantly recognizes it as a Chi-Com, reviews their dismal past history, and sends the message that it can be ignored: it'll be a dud.

Wrong.

The explosion from the grenade blows Dave up and out of his hole, out into the open where the tracers play. He is stunned and disoriented for a few seconds, but the feral part of him orders him to get small out there in the open, and he does. As he gains his senses he begins to take stock. He can tell that his back and neck are pocked with an irregular pattern of shrapnel, which feels like hot needles (he still carries some in his neck today), but he knows immediately that none of his wounds are life-threatening. Something worse has happened as a result of the crappy Chi-Com, however. His perfectly fitted jungle fatigue pants have been blown off. He has a shredded green T-shirt, he has his webbed belt around his waist, and he has his boots. That's it. *Completely* pissed off about this, Dave gets back into the hole and finishes directing the firefight. When it is over, the medic sent to care for Dave finds him stomping around bare-ass, ranting and raving—not about the stupid Chi-Com grenade that picked *this* time to explode, but about how hard it is to find a decent tailor out in the friggin' boonies.

An arc-light B-52 bombing mission inundated a ridgeline in the highlands with several strings of thousand-pound bombs. Grunts as far as a klick away felt their feet go to sleep from the thunderous shock waves vibrating out from the center of the firestorm. Giant hardwoods, huge boulders, and *anything* man-made have been uprooted and pulverized. The string of large craters becomes a dusty strip of the moon, barren and hard, devoid of life. Almost. Moving along a little-used trail just below the military crest of the ridgeline was a company of NVA. It was late in the day, their recon had reported no enemy nearby, and they were relaxed as they covered the ground quietly, eyes and weapons ready for quick response, but relaxed.

Then came a sudden pressure change and an impossible fire-and-steel typhoon, which turned their world into a howling, roaring cauldron of disintegrating death. The slowly moving green snake made of NVA soldiers that wound its way along the trail was there; then it was *not* there. The ones gifted with a micro-second of awareness and comprehension saw a force erupt around them that no one and nothing could withstand. Living men became wet distended bags of flesh and bone shards, twists of burnt tissue, blobs of bloody mucus and fat. The dreams, desires, and personalities of almost seventy men evaporated in the rising ball of fire, and for many minutes the all-powerful and never-ending jungle lay shocked, stunned, and silent after the storm. The NVA company was gone. Almost. When the American grunts reached the area of the arc light they walked right up on the last representative of the NVA unit.

He was a good-looking specimen, healthy and fit, big for a Viet, with muscular forearms and broad shoulders. He was well equipped, with ruck and web-gear, some kind of Chinese jungle boots, a soft green cap with red star, and a new AK-47, clean and locked and loaded. He sat on the jagged stump of a large tree, his AK across his lap, his feet crossed at the ankles. He waited for the Americans in silence, his eyes staring curiously at something odd very far away, a wet line of spittle falling from one corner of his compressed lips. There was no way of knowing where his place had been among the moving line of his comrades when the bombs arrived. He might have been their point, or a flanking man perhaps. Maybe he had been strolling along right in the middle of the company, a song in his heart and a smile on his lips.

He did not resist when his weapon was gently pulled from his shaking hands, and he carried himself in mute, if slightly confused, dignity as he was carefully put on a Huey and choppered out of there.

Three grunts are ordered to occupy an old sandbagged bunker on the perimeter of the firebase at An Khe. They are supposed to be on guard during the night, but have barely settled when they are beset by foraging and ferocious rats. The rats were so big. How big were they? So big they used empty sandbags to haul away the food they stole. They were not intimidated by noise, hurled boots, swinging entrenching tools, or flaming balls of C-4. The grunts fought the rats bravely for almost three hours, losing some snacks, some gear, and a little skin. Finally, after one particularly clumsy rat became entangled in the nonregulation hair of the senior grunt, the men came unglued.

All three un-assed the bunker—"Fuck it, don't give a *shit* who sees us walking away from the perimeter, don't give a *shit* what our bullshit orders are"—and moved in a stumbling cluster toward the platoon sergeant's bunker. In his mind the platoon sergeant was enjoying a minute inspection of the bass boat he intended to buy when the three grunts made their awkward entrance and began blurting out their tale of woe. The platoon sergeant could not believe his tired goddamned Army ears. The three shitbirds couldn't stay on guard in the bunker because of some pissant *rats*? How shall we say this? He gave them a severe talking-to? He read them the riot act? He chewed their sorry asses? All three. Then he sent them tumbling *out* of his bunker with the absolutely *clear* orders to get their shredded butts back to the bunker and *stay* there until relieved at O-dark-thirty.

The grunts mumbled some things the sergeant pretended

not to hear and turned toward the bunker. At that moment a very pretty pattern of VC 82mm mortars fell with a thundering and sustained roar that rent the night air and punched at the lungs of anyone in the area. It was a tight and carefully sighted and directed pattern, right on top of the rat-infested but unmanned bunker. Some VC recon team had scoped it out over the period of several days, had sighted it in, had carefully measured the distance, and had given it to the mortar crew. The crew had done a fine job, accurately placing every one of the explosions directly on or very near the bunker. Their mission lasted less than two minutes, and they were hugging the tubes and juggling their other gear as they beat a hasty retreat through the already falling counterbattery fires coming from the American base.

After it was clear that the mortar attack was over, the three grunts stood up and brushed themselves off. Then they slowly walked to the remains of the bunker and shook their heads in amazement. The bunker had first collapsed, then been blown to pieces by the falling mortars. Had they stayed at their posts, had they remained inside the bunker, they would most certainly have been dead. The bunker was now a crater surrounded by bits of wood, bent shards of metal, and shreds of burlap, hazy with smoke and dust, heavy with the smell of sulfur and cordite.

One of the grunts, told by his mom through the years to always look for the silver lining, opined, "Well, at least the VC did us a favor and exterminated those lousy rats." But as he said it a big shaggy rodent with a long and obscenely nude tail crawled matter-of-factly out of the wreckage, gave them a look, and sauntered away carrying a can of ham and eggs.

Chuck is the assistant gunner on a twin-fifty mount on a Mike-boat in the Delta. It is a hot and clear day, and the brown muddy water of the river parts at their bow and froths at their stern as the props dig in for a turn and another run along a section of the river alive with machine-gun, RPG, and AK fire. The VC have ambushed a line of five boats hauling troops and supplies to an advanced firebase; one boat has been disabled and all the boats are returning fire, Navy and Army guys are wounded, there are no gunships available, artillery fire is falling too far inland and needs to be adjusted, and it looks like the VC have things going their way.

The twin-fifty mount puts out a lot of heavy and effective firepower, the fifty-caliber machine gun being arguably the best gun ever built. Two mounted together really carry a punch, and the gunner is putting the twin stream of rounds right into the tangled scrub along the water's edge where the enemy fire is heaviest. The assistant gunner helps the gunner track and train, but he stays busiest feeding the hungry beast. Ammo. The fifties need their ammo and the AG must keep it coming so there are no pauses in the gunner's deadly tattoo. So far the boat has taken a few hits forward, but none around the fifty mount, and the enemy fire finally seems to be slacking off. Chuck bends to reach for another can of ammo, pulls it close, unlatches it, and stands next to the gunner for the reload. Except the gunner is no longer there. He has been blown out of the tub and lies sprawled and bloody on the aft deck, his body impossibly twisted and torn, most of his head gone. Chuck takes in that reality in an instant. Then he shoulders up to the guns, charges them, and caresses the triggers. He rakes the shoreline, and twice sees enemy soldiers—pulling back from their ambush positions—tumble and fall as his heavy rounds tear into them.

Chuck was proud to be promoted from AG to Gunner, but he told almost no one how it came to be.

*   *   *

A Huey clattered westbound at low altitude along Highway 19 on some ash-and-trash mission. Walking through the scattered trees and scrub brush not far from the road were two VC with AK-47's. The younger one, hardly eighteen, pulled his weapon up and around sharply as the American helicopter flew past. Almost without thinking, and knowing the older man with him would be angry and frightened of the consequences, he jerked the trigger and fired off a burst of three bullets. Then, grinning insanely, he took off at a dead run through the brush on the heels of his fleeing comrade.

One of the rounds hit a hydraulic line above the cabin of the Huey. The pilot immediately felt the loss of pressure and saw the warning light on the panel. Almost without thinking he and the co-pilot, working as twins, let the chopper descend right onto the roadway below. They got out and inspected the damage, were pleased at the quick arrival of a group of artillerymen from a near firebase (I was one of them) who took up security positions, and then waited for a Chinook to come lift them out of there. No one was hurt, and the young VC who brought the bird down probably never learned of his victory.

The infantry company was in a position on top of a blasted ridgeline. The very ground had been reduced by explosions to a gray powder, and felled trees and branches scattered everywhere made it difficult to walk, difficult to find a place to dig a fighting hole. The trees left standing were no more than naked trunks, jagged and broken at the tops, holed and splintered in the middles. The tree trunks were so full of heavy artillery and bomb shrapnel they could not be cut down; chain saws flew apart in the attempt. There was no natural cover from the relentless sun, and the ridge was covered with a patchwork of dusty green ponchos strung up to provide some meager shade.

Into this bleak landscape descended a Huey. It barely touched down long enough for the grunts on the ground to reach in and grab the resupply of ammo, smoke grenades, medical gear, and mail. Two new replacements climbed off too; then the rotor pitch changed, the nose dipped, and the Huey began to lift off to clatter out of there.

The two new soldiers stood in the dusty whirlwind while all the grunts knelt with their backs turned and their eyes closed. One of the new guys, a little sharper than the other, saw through the haze a nearby hole partially covered with a stretched poncho. Three radio antennas stuck out of the hole, and the new guy correctly guessed he'd find an officer there— or *someone* in charge he could report to. He stepped off in that direction. His jungle fatigues were a rich green, his boots shiny black. His gear gleamed in the sunlight, so new. His un-lined, open, pale boyish face gleamed, too.

The Huey rose about twelve feet into the air, drifting slightly to the right, and the rotor blade struck one of the pale and naked tree trunks filled with steel. The blades immedi-ately disintegrated into crackling shards of metal and ex-ploded outward in a razor hail. The Huey turned on its side and fell. It did not explode on impact, but lay broken and crushed in smoke, dust, debris, and noise. Both pilots were battered and bruised. The high-side door gunner wrenched his back. The crew chief broke a leg. That was all.

That was all, except for a piece of splintered rotor blade about two feet long and three inches thick, with jagged ends. It cut into the new guy just below his shoulders, dead center in his back, tore right through the rib cage—heart, lungs, all the little pumps and airbags and stuff—and came out carrying the sternum with it. The new guy may have been preparing to salute when the shard cut into him, or maybe his arms began to lift involuntarily, the way John F. Kennedy's did, I don't know. He kept his back straight as he sank to his knees. Then he gave a little cough, a bubble of blood came out of his mouth, his eyes widened, and he slowly fell onto his side. Dead.

He had been in-country one week.

The village appears deserted. There are no dogs, chickens, pigs, or villagers. No VC, either, as far as we can tell. We walk through, checking this hootch, that hole, that bunker, this well. Everything is in good repair, but deserted. Abandoned. For the past few days we have been taking the occasional sniper round as we move through the area, one or two booby traps, and not much more. We're sweeping this village half-heartedly, tired, hot, bored. Four of us move around a grass hootch and for a moment are separated from the rest of the unit.

We hear him behind us. To one of us it sounds as if he actually says *"Yeah"* or *"Oh . . .* yeah" as he comes up out of his hole. *He* is a VC snugged into a standing spider hole, waiting for us to pass. He *has* waited, and now we are in perfect position for him to rake us with his AK. We won't even have a chance to fully turn or dive to the ground, and he will waste us big-time. Except he doesn't have an AK; he has a grenade, an *American* grenade that will most definitely explode and blow us to shit, *if* it doesn't just shred us with shrapnel. Either way, we are fucked. This all registers in that instant when he stands, pushes the grass-and-bamboo cover away, and lobs the grenade.

Except he doesn't lob the grenade.

With our all-seeing all-knowing real-close-to-dying eyes we see he has already pulled the pin. Now we see his fingers open so the spoon handle can *ping* away, and here it comes ready to explode. I have to say this now, okay? The poor little VC throws like a girl—I mean, he *would* have thrown like a girl. That's how he looked with his elbow pointing at us, his hand filled with the grenade lying all the way back on his bent wrist. But he bobbled it. It slipped out of his hand; he caught it with the other; then it tumbled again. Each time he reached for it the grenade slipped further down his front, his chest, then his belly, then down toward his crotch where we couldn't see. Each time he made a grab for it he let out a little grunt, like, "Uh . . . uh . . . *uh*." His last grunt was very loud and made through clenched teeth, and there came a pause in real time as he argued with himself: keep trying to reach the grenade and throw it, or forget it and wiggle out of that hole most ricky-tick.

The explosion of the grenade felt very contained and powerful to the four of us eating Viet village dirt a few feet away. There was a leaping gout of smoke and flame from the hole, and a rippling shock wave. One would have expected the VC to do a Roman candle up and out of the hole, to become a VC bottle-rocket, as it were. Instead he remained in the hole, spinning and jerking demonically like a whirling dervish in a blender. He finally writhed and bumped to a stop, his lips stretched back from his teeth, his hair sticking up in spikes, his eyes bulging. Then, much like the witch of the west, he sank out of sight.

The four of us who witnessed this slowly got to our feet, dusted ourselves off, checked our weapons, took two steps, and began to laugh. We were alive, he was dead, and the whole thing was ridiculous. We laughed, laughed until we were weak and went down on one knee, laughed with an intensity that bordered on hysteria. The others in the unit found us like that, sort of laughing almost crying hiccupping coughing, and unable to get to our feet and move out.

Capricious and deadly, the whole sorry and wasteful business.

Despoil

I HAD to piss real bad.

Had been laying up under some scrub bushes a few yards from a curving trail in the triple canopy west of Kontum all through the long wet night. Was with a reinforced squad-sized ambush, set out to interdict enemy resupply activity. It had been a very quiet, very hot, very nerve-racking night filled with unrealized anticipatory dread. Watched, listened, dozed. Quietly stretched, quietly sipped from my canteen, quietly picked my nose. Thought about home, thought about dying, thought about girls. Strained my eyeballs into the sooty shadows looking for the wily ghost-soldiers who were my enemy. Discovered I had to piss in the wee hours, the darkest, loneliest, most-popular-with-poets hours.

Problem. You're lying in a semifetal position on your side, your M-16 locked and loaded under your fingertips. You can't just stand, stretch, and tell the other guys you gotta go see a man about a horse, gotta take a whiz, gotta take a leak. No way. You *could* carefully unbutton the fatigue trouser fly, reach in and find your poor shriveled penis—all that's left after the wee-hours hard-on actuated by those thoughts of girls—and urinate where you lie. You would try to scrunch back away from the puddle, of course, and hope it didn't run downhill into your boots. Or you could grit your teeth, think about other things, and wait out the dawn.

They gave me other things to thing about. Dawn came. The rising mists diffused the edges of leaves and tree trunks, but the trail could clearly be seen. Down the trail came their point man. They had a point with an AK, a trail man with an AK, and between them four bicycle couriers. The point man actually ambled, his AK lying on his shoulder like he was some coon hunter on his way home. We let him go by.

The team I was with had stiffened at the first sight of the NVA. No one breathed, no one moved. We waited. The coon hunter ambled past, the first biker came into view. He had an SKS rifle tied to the handlebars, and he walked beside the bike, on the left side. He used a stick to extend the handlebar on that side and help him balance the large bag of rice tied to the bike. He had a soft cap down over his eyes, and he was staring only at his feet on the trail. Behind him came the other three, each the same, but wearing their caps on the back of the head or on a string around the throat, looking up into the trees, at the back of the man in front of them, or intently all around the jungle in nervous search for us.

Two of us pitched grenades onto the trail as their last man, no bike, scanning eyes, AK at the ready, came into view. We sprang the ambush with gritted teeth, hoarse yells, and a tear-ing roaring fire from our M-16's and the M-60. The NVA soldiers leapt into a writhing spastic dance, arms flung, heads back, mouths open. Their point man dropped his AK and scampered up the trail out of sight and away. Their trail guy came swift and deadly, with his AK barking and ripping toward us, his knees bent slightly, his eyes bright through the smoke. It was only dumb luck that kept us from being hit by his fire, and he died in a twisting and doubling convulsion as we ripped him.

Murder in the morning takes only a few seconds, and so it was with this. We got up, did a cautious recon up and down the trail, saw no additional threat, and examined our work. Three of the bicycle couriers had probably died before they hit the ground. One looked like he wanted to ride away, his body squatting on the frame of his bike. Two had flung their bikes as they fell, and stared openmouthed at the trees over-head and beyond. The fourth was still alive in the middle of the trail. He had been hit in the torso and legs, and at least once in the head, but it didn't seem to affect his form. He did a perfect freestyle in the dirt, kicking his feet rhythmically, turning his head back and forth, lifting one arm forward, pulling down with cupped hand, then following with the other arm and hand. His hands actually cut grooves in the trail, he tried so hard, and his broken body inched forward as he grunted in effort. We didn't have a lot of time to stand around watching, but we did. Drops of morning moisture fell through the heat onto broad green leaves, insects hummed, his hands made a scraping sound in the dirt. Someone made a comment about Johnny Weissmuller, someone else timed him. He finished his race after one and one-half minutes, racking himself with a final sobbing breath, then shrinking into the dirt to become very still.

We smashed their SKS rifles against tree trunks to ruin them. We went through their packs. We took their AK's. We cut open the large bags of rice, stuck in grenades, dove for cover, and were showered with the precious kernels. The dead NVA on the trail were coated with the stuff, which made them look like hosts for instant maggots. We had to go, but we had to deny food to our enemy, so we spent a few minutes scattering it around in the dirt and loam. I solved my problem just before we turned to melt back into the green.

I sighed deeply with relief as I pissed into the rice.

Smoke

My friend Dave came across probably the unluckiest NVA soldier sent south by the revered and grossly in-
competent General Giap. Dave was a two-niner like me, and
Artillery Forward Observer. He was assigned to the grunt
units of the Fourth Infantry Division—the Ivy League. He
spent lots of time in the Dak To area when it was hot, picked
up a couple of Hearts, and managed to get through it and
come home.

One day he was out for a walk in the park with the grunts,
and the point element thought they had movement somewhere in the green to their front. Wanting to play it safe, the
grunt lieutenant asked Dave to prepare to bring down some
artillery fire if it broke loose. Dave was already giving the
grids to the battery covering their AO, and asked for a smoke
round to adjust from.

The 105 or 155mm artillery smoke round had a metal base
plate that separated from the casing before the smoke was ig-

nited. The plate weighed about a pound, was maybe six inches in diameter, and had no function once it separated. Dave called for and got one smoke round, which deployed above them and to their front, and from it Dave was ready to call in the high explosives when necessary. After a moment's pause the point signaled that they were apparently mistaken. They had no movement, nothing, and the sweaty hump through the jungle could resume. No further artillery would be called for.

The grunts had moved forward less than a hundred yards when point put the unit down on one knee again and signaled for the LT to come up. Dave went with him. The cluster of grunts on the trail shuffled apart as they approached, and then they saw the unluckiest NVA soldier ever sent south by the visionary Uncle Ho.

He was an honest-to-Giap NVA troop, all right. Had the racing slicks on his feet, dark green pants, light green shirt; had the khaki-colored pith helmet, which probably protects the wearer from falling piths. He also had an AK-47, a ruck filled with maps, and a photograph of a smiling young Vietnamese woman. The NVA's pith helmet had *not* protected him from a falling artillery base-plate, which had come waffling out of the sky, Frisbee'd through the upper branches of the trees, and hit the soldier on top of his pith-helmeted head. It brained him, just like that.

Dave said they stared at him sprawled there facedown in the middle of the trail, and shook their heads in disbelief that some poor bastard could be so unlucky. It was unlikely he had been strolling along out there alone, so apparently whatever troops were with him didi'd when the smoke round deployed and their fellow freedom fighter suddenly pitched forward to forever embrace that mother soil he fought for so bravely.

They took his equipment and left him there, the thick blob of blood coming from his mouth turning to black paste in the dirt.

Dave said he enjoyed beaucoup respect from the grunts from that day on.

Voyeur

Saw some pictures. Photographs.

Maybe it was a Phillip Caputo "Delcorso's Gallery" kind of thing—*combat* photographers obtaining credentials and inserting themselves and their cameras into war. Maybe they had no feelings one way or the other about the politics of war or the meaning of war, but simply had the desire to freeze pieces of it, document it, capture it on film for display. Maybe they had plenty of feelings—let's make them altruistic, God-and-man-loving feelings about the horror, futility, and crime of the thing called war—and attempted to capture on film a tableau so horrific that once viewed it would cause the immediate cessation of all war. Maybe they were out to make a buck and get some kicks doing manly things at the same time. I don't know. I *do* know I could not shed the feeling that they were perverted and obscene voyeurs.

Saw some photographs in black-and-white. (Black-and-white equals stark, hard-edged, unforgiving, gritty, real.) They were in a book of photographs taken by *combat* photographers in Vietnam. The NVA had fired their rockets into a town marketplace. This was before smart bombs and rockets. These rockets were sort of pointed, sort of elevated, then fired into the general area. Sometimes they actually killed *soldiers* or blew up *military* equipment.

One photograph (it was in stark black-and-white) showed a part of the marketplace that had been hit by the exploding rocket. In it a young Vietnamese boy stands looking down at his dead mother. The boy has been horribly wounded, his right arm and shoulder burnt beyond third degree, the right side of his torso shredded by the blast and shrapnel. General Giap's gallant and wily soldiers, the NVA, scored a great military victory by blowing up the marketplace and killing the woman and wounding her young son, and the hardened veteran *combat* photographer was there—*right there*—to capture the moment in brutal and truth-revealing black-and-white.

When I looked at the photograph taken in stark black-and-white by the gallant *combat* photographer and saw that horribly wounded boy grimacing down at his dead mother, I saw on *this* side of the photo the *actual combat photographer*. And do you know what he was doing as the horribly wounded boy stood there staring down at his dead mother? Why, the *combat* photographer was taking the boy's picture. You know what I think? I think the little boy died from his wounds. I'm only guessing, because the accompanying text doesn't make it clear, but in looking at his wounds—and having *seen* a few wounds—I don't think he lived. But the last few moments of the boy's life were enriched by the fact that a *combat* photographer documented his pain. Did the photographer act out of a desire to educate the ignorant back home? Out of a desire to end all war? Out of a desire to win peer-group awards and sell his stark and brutal black-and-white photo to some wire service or magazine so somebody else could sell advertisements?

The warrior kind of Vietnam vet like me saw the photograph, knew the *combat* photographer stood there taking a picture of the boy, and wondered why the silly mercenary son of a bitch didn't just put his camera down and help the child. What if it was just a few soothing and kind words, even if from a foreigner, even if there *was* nothing anyone could do to save his life or the life of his mother? Could have grabbed a first-aid kit (It's morphine, my child. Have a little sleep now before the big sleep, dream of sitting with your mother in cool green grass under a reaching shade tree. . . .), grabbed a blanket, grabbed the boy's one good hand and held tightly, could have *done* something for the child.

Not surprisingly, you know what is visible in the upper right-hand corner of the photograph? Another camera aimed at the boy's stunned and uncomprehending face. Our *combat* photographer was almost scooped by some other hero with a camera. Both of these samaritans stood there focusing and clicking away while the boy staggered in agony, fear, and confusion. I guess what they did was so important neither one could put down his camera for a moment.

I saw the photograph years after the war. It was in a collection of shots taken by *combat* photographers who were later killed. Perhaps this somehow validates them and their work, I don't know. When I decided to look back into the green, that photograph came to mind. When I was young and in Vietnam, I paid no attention to journalists or photographers—they were completely superfluous. Nonentities. They were not the only ones with cameras, of course. We, as young soldiers in a foreign land engulfed in war, pointed our Instamatics at the water buffalo, mist-wreathed mountains, bullet-pocked churches, and dead enemy soldiers. They were photos of *our* war; we didn't sell them. We either sent them home to be stuffed into eventually forgotten photo albums, or threw them away. They were for *us*, not for sale.

Howl now, injured journalist. Thrust that indignant jaw out of the trough and tell us about being a *combat* photographer, a *combat* reporter, about *being* there. Yeah, right. Now go read what your boy Michael Herr has to say about it. You flew in, you flew out, like posturing parasitic paparazzi who crashed the wake of someone they didn't know so they could eat the food and take the pennies from his eyes. War, and all that it does to us, is too personal to be stared at by your cyclopean eye.

A wiggling mass of pale wet maggots going about their grisly work is repulsive to us, but we understand that at least *they* have some purpose in this world.

Green Machine

I THINK even the guys who absolutely hated the Army will admit that though it was mostly screwed-up, there were moments when it showed a clumsy kind of caring. The mail was a biggie, those letters from home. The Army tried hard to bring you the mail, no matter where you were, no matter what was going on at the time.

"*Hey*, you stupid dink NVA shitheads! Can't you knock off all the damned shooting and mortaring and stuff and let a man at least sit down for a couple of minutes to read a *letter*?"

Holidays were another sphere in which the Army made an effort, even though it seemed to always create the opposite effect of the one hoped for. They did it with food. Thanksgiving dinner, soup-to-nuts, by God. At Fort Dix the officers of my Advanced Infantry Training company wore their dress blues, had their wives on their arm, and helped serve up the turkey and dressing. We had the dinner in the mess hall, which was decorated with paper turkeys and pumpkins. You never saw such a glum bunch sitting there.

Thanksgiving came for me next year in the Highlands. I was with a leg unit, out humping the boonies, and word was a *hot meal* would be choppered out to us. There would be turkey, stuffing, mashed potatoes, greens, coffee, pie, and even ice cream. It was *the word*, and we clung to it. Damned Army was gonna do it right, we said, actually gonna get us a hot meal out here in Dinkland. Can you believe it?

I think they were called Marmite containers, the green metal coolers they carried food to the field in. Somehow they had some Hueys and they loaded them up with all the containers, turkey in this one, pie in that one, mashed potatoes over there. The choppers lifted and spread out in search of their hungry flock, somewhere down there in the green. They spent the better part of Thanksgiving Day flying turkey deliveries, and it probably seemed like a cool thing to do.

Ours finally came thudding in during the late afternoon. We had gone to ground in a good spot, marked the LZ, had the bird on the radio, and waited. Three or four grunts were detailed to stand by, and when the Huey hovered in they ran out to grab the goodies. It went smoothly, with the Huey getting in and out with no time wasted, no time-as-target. The jungle became quiet again as the bird left, and hungry hands reached for the Marmite containers full of that U.S. Army Turkey Day feast.

Ice Cream.

We were the recipients of five each MIAI, OD in color, magazine-fed, center-fire, containers-food-metal—each dutifully packed with five gallons of vanilla ice cream. We stared at it in silence, each of us aware of the *certainty* of it all. I think we all shrugged in unison as we thought, "Of *course*." That was the end of the hump for that day. We dug into the vanilla ice cream with our bare and dirty hands, smearing and wolfing it, digging into it quick before it turned to white mud in the heat. It tasted great and we enjoyed the hell out of it, but many of us got sick to our stomachs later, so we dug in for a quiet night of Thanksgiving reflection.

We were pleased to hypothesize that somewhere out there in the green, out there in the highland boonies, was a grunt line unit in possession of five Marmite containers of mashed potatoes.

Regrets

THE Army bureaucracy and coincidence teamed up to clobber my old man during my tour. Somewhere during my last operation attached to some unit out in the boonies, and my first hospital stay in Pleiku, the Army concluded I was missing. They decided to inform my family of this. Never mind that I had specifically indicated on a personal information form that I did *not* want this to happen; they fired off one of those bleak and terrible telegrams that say too much and too little. It stated I was "missing in action," whereabouts unknown, further information to follow if ascertained.

During the same week my Recon and RTO, not knowing how long I'd be hospitalized, decided to ship a few of my things home for safekeeping. They were constantly on the move, couldn't carry my stuff with them, and knew I would probably send it home at the end of my tour anyway. Into a box they threw an extra pair of boots, a camouflaged poncho liner, a beret, some Yard bracelets, some photos, a broken watch, and a couple of other things. They included an awk-

ward and laconic note, which said something like "The Lieutenant is a great guy and here is some of his stuff," taped it up
nicely, and sent it home.

The telegram and the box of "personal effects" arrived
within a day of each other. There was no further information,
no explanation, no way for my parents to follow up. They
read the telegram over and over looking for nuances they
might have missed. They gently sifted through the box of
stuff, searching for reassurance. Then they looked at each
other.

I'm told my old man went out the front door and sat on
the front step. He stayed right there four days, four nights.
He didn't speak to anyone, get up, or go anywhere. He simply sat quietly, smoking his Camels and staring out across the
yard. He appeared unaware of life going on around him, paid
no attention to the comings and goings of others, and seemed
to quicken slightly only on the approach of the mailman.
Four day, four nights.

Finally the Army determined what I knew all along. I was
not "missing." I was not even "in action." I was getting the
shit kicked out of me by a mosquito, but otherwise I was still
doing my two-niner thing in the Nam. With a flourish and
the quiet sense of a job well done, the Army sent off another
telegram, advising my parents of this discovery. My Recon
and RTO were glad I was back with them; they told me of the
stuff they sent home, and we thought no more about it.

Four day, four nights. My old man never said a word to me
about them, and I only heard of them years after he died. He
told my mom the hours just before dawn were the hardest.

Midnight Requisition

THROUGH much of my time in Vietnam I worked with two enlisted men. They weren't always the same two, but they were of the same rank, held the same jobs, and helped form our team. All the clearly positive old-war-movie characters, cut from the mold of decency, loyalty, skill, and courage—the sergeant who sticks with his officer through thick and thin, the quiet tough ones who are right there when they must be, the ones who have a girl back home and a never-stated but deep love of country. They were my Recon and RTO.

The Recon I worked most with was a big redheaded sunburned guy with a bushy mustache, lots of strength built into his large frame, and a quiet patience in times of stress. He was a Topanga Canyon, California, kind of kid who couldn't wait to get back to his life in the World. He talked about his mom and cars, never much about what we were doing there in the Nam. A young man smart enough to play the military games effortlessly.

The RTO I spent the most time with was from New York, the heart of the Big Apple, the "only real city in the world." He was a wise guy, snappy, cigarette hanging, grin challenging, eyes looking for any chance of mischief. He had his ups and downs with the Army way of life, and came to me in tenuous standing. He took care of me, though, during the little base-camp time we had and out in the boonies. He got along well with Recon, played it straight with me as his LT, and deserved more in the end than I was able to secure for him. With his checkered background (military *and* civilian) he was a natural scrounger.

"RTO," I might say, "we could use more M-16 bandoliers, two more PRC-25 radio batteries, and more socks."

"Yeah. Okay, Lieutenant. Be back in about an hour."

"RTO, we need a new PRC-10 and a new PRC-25, and see if you can get us a bloop gun and some ammo, and two cases of Dr Pepper and some Miller beer for you and Recon."

"Sure, no problem, LT. I should be back by lunchtime."

"RTO, the jeep we got is gettin' raggedy. We need some new wheels. I wouldn't mind having two new M-60's and our very own APC [armored personnel carrier] either. And, boy, would I like to get my hands on a chilled bottle of Châteauneuf du Pape, two blond strippers, and a king-size bed."

"You want it, you got it, LT. I'll have to take Recon with me, and we might not be back till tomorrow mornin', okay?"

(He actually did show up once with an APC. We called it our own for about a week until the unit it belonged to—all huffy and indignant—demanded it back.)

While attached to the 3rd ARVN Armored on Highway 14, we lived in a sandbagged hootch within the ARVN's compound. It was a couple of klicks north of "the hill," the big artillery camp at Pleiku. We were attached to various units, but loosely parented to an ARTY headquarters unit there. We even had a land-line in place so we could use one of those hand-crank telephones to call in our H&I (harassment and interdiction) fires. Because we were always on the move, resupply and upkeep of equipment was a problem. I cranked up the land line one day, spoke with the colonel, told him I needed a bunch of stuff, and got his impatient response. The colonel was from the *old* guard, by God. He had been a shave-tail in the *Big One* and a captain in Korea. He had been part of This Man's Army when it was *tough*, hear me?

"Look, McDonald," he barked, "you got a couple of buck sergeants workin' for ya, don't ya, kid? Send their ass out on the little . . . uh . . . *requisition* mission, capiche? Let them walk through where the pickings are good and fill up your resupply order so you can get on with the business of killing gooks. Got it?"

So I gave RTO and Recon my shopping list, glanced nervously at their conspiratorial grins of anticipation, and sent them toward the hill. They returned in a couple of hours, tired, happy, and excited.

"Check it out, Lieutenant, check it *out*—"

"Yeah, man. New seat covers for the jeep, covers for *both* radios, a shitload of new batteries. Even two new whip antennas for the PRC-10, and two for the 25."

"Hey, LT, get a load of this little floating compass that sticks to the dash of the jeep. Is that cool, or what?"

"See the ammo? Got lots of bandoliers, too, and that bloop gun you been dreamin' about."

"Holy shit," I said, pushing on the seats. "You guys even got new seat cushions for this ride, and I *love* that fancy rawhide steering-wheel cover—"

"Cast your eyes on the cases of beer, LT, *and* the bags of pretzels from the World, *and* the issues of *Playboy* and *Field & Stream*."

"Wow," said I, "you guys did good."

We were sucking the beers, thumbing through the *Playboys*, and munching the pretzels when a nervous little ring came from the land line. I was closest, and picked it up.

"That's *my* shit!" yelled the voice on the other end of the static. "'Scuse me?" I responded.

"Goddammit, McDonald!" yelled the colonel. "I'll have your *ass*, and the asses of those two thieves you sent over here to the hill!"

"What?"

"My driver saw your two sergeants as they were leaving, *Lieutenant*. Don't play dumb with me. You sent those two scroungers out lookin', and *they took my shit*."

"But—"

"'But,' my ass! My seatcovers, my *cushions*, even my custom-made rawhide steering-wheel cover my wife sent me, you bastards! My little compass! My *Field & Stream* magazines—"

"What about the *Playboys*?"

"Don't get smart with me, McDonald. Goddamned sons a bitches comin' up here and stealin' my shit? You gotta be kidding me!" He stopped, I could hear his heavy breathing low-crawling down the length of wire strung in the ditch alongside Highway 14. He sniffed and launched himself again. "My pretzels! My *pretzels*. Do you know how hard it is to get those Pennsylvania kinda pretzels in this fucking dump, Lieutenant?"

"Um . . . *difficult*, Colonel . . . sir?"

"You tell those two felons you've got hangin' out with you to load my stuff back into that sorry jeep of yours and hightail it back up to this hill *pronto* and *right now*. I'll be busy in the

TOC, and none of my guys will see anything. You got it? Have them bring my stuff back now and that'll be the end of it."

"Yessir," said I.

"And, McDonald," added the colonel in an easier, almost plaintive tone, "next time you send those two out hunting, tell 'em to go to the *Engineer* compound or the *grunts'* HQ, or better yet over to the fucking *Air Force* base down the road. Understand?"

"Yessir. Got it. Will do. They'll be bringing it back now."

"I want my little compass," said the colonel with a laugh. "And my custom-made rawhide steering-wheel cover, and what's left of my pretzels, *and* my copies of *Field & Stream*. You shitbirds can keep the rest."

"Yessir," said I.

Beaucoup
Din Ky Dao

HE had discovered the intricacies, intent, and effectiveness of the "mad minute." I stood in the flat early sunlight, my boots in the red dust of the perimeter around the compound, looking him over. He had made it to within ten or fifteen yards of our inner wire before it began. CO's of units in night positions would often call for a mad minute in those elastic moments between false dawn and the real thing. It was a way to shake up and wake up the men, a way to check the weapons, a way to flex your muscles and get the adrenaline pumping, and a truly American way to say, "Gooood morning, Viet*nam*."

"On my count," would intone the conductor of the mad minute. "Three, two, one . . . mike-mike . . . mike-mike . . ."

Every weapon on the perimeter of the compound—machine guns, automatic rifles, bloop guns, occasionally the mortar tubes, maybe a recoilless if there was one—would open fire into their sector of the wire and cleared approaches. It was a roaring, hellacious, frightening expenditure of firepower, concentrated and deadly. There always seemed to be a maniacal glee associated with it, as if all the pent-up fears collected during the long night had to be let out of the bag and you were damned glad to see them go. On occasion I felt quite sure that if I looked over my shoulder during the mad minute I'd see a squad of high school cheerleaders from the World, bright in their short skirts and sweaters with the school colors, great legs, sparkling eyes, and convincing smiles. They would be waving their pom-poms and shouting, "Push 'em back, push 'em back . . . waaaay *back*!"

The Vietcong soldier I stood over had approached the perimeter cautiously through the scrub until he got to the cleared area next to the wire. Then he had gone to his belly to wiggle through the different strands of wire and trip flares, as only a good VC sapper could do. He had only one more strand to go before he was right up against the edge. What then? Was he simply gathering intelligence, looking and listening to what the bulky, smelly, clumsy Americans had to say in the morning? Was he a point man for an upcoming attack, scoping our defenses while laying wire or setting charges? Was he a real sapper, with a satchel full of explosives, intent on finding our TOC or mess area and blowing up a bunch of us along with himself? There was no way to tell.

I stared at him. He probably had not read Remarque's *All Quiet on the Western Front*, so he would not know why I thought he resembled a soldier described in a passage from that book. (Am I being judgmental, prejudiced, and condescending when I say he probably hadn't read it? You bet. I don't think the dumb son of a bitch read it, okay?) He was extremely dead. Dead as only a stupid VC who died in the wire during a mad minute can be. He appeared to be praying, with his shoulders straight, his forearms coming together with his palms flattened against each other at the top. His face was lifted up, empty eyes beseeching the infinite for forgiveness or explanation. Most of the back of his skull was gone; it looked like an empty fur-lined coconut. From his shoulders back he was mostly gone also, cut to bloody ribbons by the fire, his shoulders, face, and forearms held in place by that last strand of wire. On the Western Front the soldier praying in the wire was there for only a moment, then was completely shot away. This guy had managed to hang in there, probably quite taken with the eccentric and martial ways of those crazy Americans.

I decided I was late for a very important date with a pleasantly odd milliner, and hurried back for a nice hot cup of tea.

Promise

I HAVE no doubt some moviemaker would film the sequence in slow motion. That way the girl's eyes could be captured as they moved to follow mine, the wisps of hair curling around her ears could be seen to flutter in the breeze, her black and white ao dai would flow away from her legs like a streamer, behind the minibus. Maybe slo-mo could even capture the way her smile began to broaden one millimeter at a time, a smile filled with recognition. She recognized my look of appreciation, my desire for her, the potential for us as lovers. She had the demurely smoldering look and smile of the completely self-possessed Oriental female, and she gave them to me as our lives passed on a dusty highway in the heat.

We were on our way to join some unit somewhere in central Vietnam. We waited beside a busy stretch of highway for a jeep that would take us to a nearby chopper pad. We'd been there almost an hour, and were thirsty, covered with dust, and certain we'd been forgotten. The highway had been used by heavy traffic since the engineers swept it for mines early in the morning. Traffic included U.S. and ARVN jeeps, various trucks, and the occasional tank. Mixed in with the military vehicles were the swarms of civilian people-movers— motorcycles, scooters, the occasional car, and the ubiquitous open minibus. They had the cab of a minibus, with the back open and benches on both sides. They were built to carry two in the front and maybe six or eight in back, but were often jammed to standing room only, plus people hanging off the sides. Throw on the chickens, pigs, dogs, bags, boxes, bicycles, babies, and baskets of dried fish, and you had quite the rolling spectacle. Usually these vehicles were painted in gaudy pastels, striping and piping, fuzzy dice and bongos. Most appeared to be driven by the same sour-faced Viet-namese man. He stared straight ahead, spoke in rapid and dis-approving Viet to everybody, and spit out the side window with discriminating accuracy. He wore shower shoes, black slacks, and a white shirt with a pocket protector containing three pens. He wore the expression of a man who knew he'd never reach his destination.

We stood with our gear, waiting, the sun searing down onto us, the trucks rumbling past. Then the slo-mo kicked in. Came a lull in the traffic. Came from the north, my left, headed south, a light blue minibus with the above-described driver. It had the chickens, the children, the baskets of fish, and maybe a dozen people on board, all civilians. The girl sat on the bench on the right side of the bus, her back and left shoulder to me as they puttered by. She sat on the rear edge of the bench, her left ankle wedged against the small gate at the rear. With her right hand she gripped a stanchion behind the person sitting next to her. Her left hand lay folded in her lap. She was classically beautiful. Late teens, early twenties, I'd guess, the flawless eggshell complexion, that thick gleam-ing head of black hair pulled back from her smooth forehead into a loose ponytail which hung all the way down her back. Her outfit was traditional—a tight-fitting white top, half-Chinese collar, then flowing silk panels over clinging pants.

The way she sat, back straight, very formal, very confident, caught my eye first. *Whew*, said a voice in my head as I kept my eyes on her. I looked at her shoulders, her right hand, her left arm, her hair, then the left side of her face as it turned, her eyes coming around in awareness of my examination. I almost wanted the minibus to hurry so she would appear sooner in profile, and was not disappointed when she did. Then she turned, her eyes, her face, her left shoulder. She turned her hips and looked at me, and smiled.

I know there was a roar that came with the explosion. Of course there was, a thunderous, sustained, pulsating roar that announced the detonation of a huge explosive buried in the road. Yeah, the engineers had missed it that morning, but possibly it had been masked by wood and tarmac. There would have been wires running to it, but inert, not hot. Very probably an eight-inch or 175mm artillery round. Big, whatever it was, and command-detonated: detonated on command. The wires leading to the charge trailed out from under the roadbed somewhere nearby, and there some patriotic freedom fighter—some might call him a soldier—lay in wait for what he considered a worthwhile target. This was a war, remember. He would have the wires hooked up to a charge box, and when his valuable target came along he would watch, wait, carefully gauge speed and direction, then set it off. Explode it. Detonate it on command. His command.

His command detonation in this case created an impossibly lurid and fiery charnel house in the middle of the road. There appeared a crater three feet deep and ten feet around. All of the dirt and tarmac were dug out and flung up in a dirty, dusty geyser. The minibus, too. The flimsy metal of the bus buckled in from the edges first, pulling the four wheels in against one another as the center of the vehicle mushroomed open and twisted upward like jagged metal fingers. The cab tore away from the benches, and the whole mess lifted majestically into the air about ten feet, flipped over, and fell with a clatter back into the crater.

The passengers riding the minibus did not have to worry about being crushed as it crashed down, however, because they had already been chopped, pulped, splintered, charred, melted, turned inside out, or just butchered into partially recognizable quarters. Body parts, clothing, shoes (why does it always seem there are more shoes than feet?), eyeglasses, watches, hats, toys, and engine fragments rained down onto the road and beside it for several seconds.

Stunned silence will have to suffice. There came a stunned silence, eventually broken by a machine-gunner on a nearby truck. He began firing blindly into the adjacent tree line. This set off a wild minute or two during which everybody with a weapon was shooting at the scrub brush where *he* might be. This stuttered to a halt, to be replaced by the first tentative piercing wails from small gaggles of women who had been walking alongside the road.

Thanks to the capricious nature of explosives, none of us standing only a few yards away was hurt. We were covered in clods of dirt and sheets of dust, choked by black oily smoke from two of the minibus's burning tires. Otherwise, we were okay. We looked at each other and probably croaked, "Holy *shit*," "What the *fuck*," and "Jesus H. Kee*rist*." I dusted myself off, made sure I still had my M-16, and walked toward the carnage.

I knew I would not find her, because I had seen with my own eyes how her body had separated into minute particles as she rose and disintegrated, the fragments of her melding with the rising fingers of fire. She was there, smiling at me, beckoning me, promising me, challenging me; then her gaze shifted to the sun and she lifted and became the billowing dust and ash.

I stood at the lip of the crater, let my eyes shoot quickly here and there for some sign, trying to look but not see, and spotted a fluttering piece of black silk near what might have been a small sandal. There was too much of the other, though, and I had to flee. My Recon joined me as I walked down the road toward the jeep that had finally come for us. It took a moment for me to realize that he was yelling in my ear. His voice sounded hollow.

"What the hell was *that*, LT?" he asked, his face red under the dust. "I mean, they mine the road and blow up our trucks and tanks or whatever. They leave pressure-detonated mines to blow the first thing that rolls over them, right? Or they set up a command-detonated mine so they can watch the traffic and pick a nice juicy target, yeah? A *valuable* target, something that will hurt their enemy—that's *us*—like a tank or big ammo truck or something so they can win their goddamned war, right? *Right*?"

I said nothing, too close to vomiting, too close to sitting down in the middle of the road and staring at my feet until wings grew from my heels and flew me the hell *out* of there.

"So they have their *command*-detonated mine in place," hissed Recon. "They wait, they watch, then they *command* it to blow up that bus and a bunch of just plain *people* trying to make it through their lousy day? What the fuck is *that*, LT?"

"They showed the people they still control the road," I answered.

He gazed at the traffic again rumbling past, the wrecked minibus already bulldozed aside. "Nah," he said, and spit. "They control *nothing*, they just *took* those people."

I had no more words to say, and as we left the area I wished I could see the girl's face again. No matter how hard I tried I could not make my mind picture her. Years later she returned to me, quiet and watchful, her demurely smoldering smile still challenging.

Hump

WENT up into the Laos-Cambodia-Vietnam triangle area on an operation called Tollroad. A Special Forces
team and their Montagnard company escorted a group of
U.S. engineers, not to build, but to destroy. Through this
area the Ho Chi Minh Trail was well developed and well
maintained, with cleared gravel and dirt roads, small wooden
bridges, drainage culverts, and bunkers placed here and there
in case an NVA truck driver had to bail out during an air
strike. Our job was to mess up a couple of klicks of the road,
blow the bunkers, culverts, and bridges, crater the road with
shaped charges, and block it with abatises. The Yards would
cover the shovel shooters, and I would provide ARTY and air
for the SF guys.

The choppers put us down on the east side of the road and
we went exploring. Sure enough, the NVA had cut themselves a fairly comfortable supply route through there, but
they had apparently didi'd as we approached. We were able to
go about our business unhindered. We found one old Eastern

Bloc three-quarter-ton truck pushed into a ditch, severely cannibalized for parts; some gasoline and rice stores; and a whole lot of quiet. The engineers did their thing with blocks of C-4 and det cord, and by late afternoon we had laid waste to a long section of the roadway. The route followed the natural path through a small valley between two high ridgelines, so we headed west and up to find a place for the night. There was not a doubt in anyone's mind that the wily NVA had been observing us during the day, so we moved nice and easy through the double canopy, expecting his ambush. It did not come.

It turned out to be a difficult hump for me, because of my RTO and Recon. My usual RTO had gone off on R&R. My Recon had had to leave me at the lift point because he'd come down with a major case of the greenapple quicksteps, Viet version: rice, sauce, and grit your teeth. He was pissed and did not want to leave me, but there was no way. He caught a ride back to our base with a command Loach, and gave me a wave and a forlorn look as it lifted off. Now came my problem. The operation was on, we were headed out, and I needed an RTO and Recon pronto. The artillery HQ responded in classic military fashion. When a battery CO was told to provide two men for an operation, did he send out two of his competent, motivated, squared-away troops? Yeah, right. Two minutes before we lifted off two of the sorriest-looking privates I've ever seen trudged over and advised me they were my guys. They were big-time slackers, had no use for each other, and in no way wanted to go out for a couple of days and hump the boonies, where they might have to act like soldiers.

We hadn't been on the ground more than a few minutes when they began to bicker, whining and complaining like a couple of spoiled kids. They slowed us down and got in the way; the SF lieutenant made it clear to me he didn't have time for any artillery babies, and I'd better control "my" men. In frustration, I finally took the radio from them and humped it myself, telling them to be quiet and stay away from each other. We humped it to the high ground in the late heat of day, straight up a hard ridgeline, and I got so damned tired with my gear *and* the PRC-25 I found myself scanning the ground for one of those apple-turnover-shaped toe-popper mines, thinking it would be all right if I "accidentally" stepped on one, broke a few bones in my foot, and took a dust-off out of there. But you can never find a mine when you want one, and I had to finish that bastard of a hump just like all the other happy campers.

We found a suitable night pos near the military crest of the ridge and took our SF-assigned positions inside the outer perimeter, which was manned by the Yards. I always slept in a jungle hammock. They were light and easy to pack, easy to string between trees, out of the dirt and creepy-crawlers, and cool and comfortable. Strung a mosquito bar over it, and my poncho over that. Had me a little treetop condo, no rain, heat, or bugs. Dug a shallow fighting hole under it to roll into at the first hint of incoming, and was ready for the night. The SF guys always said there were two heights to string a hammock, AK-47 height or mortar height. I tried to pick a level in between, and during all my months in the boonies never got shot or fragged in my sleep.

The two lovelies assigned to me were having problems, though, arguing about every little thing, finally getting loud and almost coming to blows over who had what for dinner. We were settling into our night pos, like I said, and that was a good time to keep *quiet*. A few seconds after their altercation began I had the SF lieutenant in my face. He told me in a hiss if I couldn't keep *my* two assholes under control and *quiet*—they were endangering the whole group—then he and his guys would take care of it and in the morning we'd call in a dust-off for two U.S. KIA's. He was absolutely dead serious, and I told him I understood. I got the two privates, told them they were dogmeat if they kept it up, and advised them to finish *whatever* they were having for dinner and settle in for the night. They nodded glumly.

Not two minutes later they were at it again, this time viciously quiet, but obviously serious. The Engineer LT sitting a few yards away gave me a low whistle and pointed. One of the privates had a bayonet pointed at the other's guts; both were in a crouch and moving around a deep fighting hole they had dug earlier out of their mutual fear of things that go bump in the night. It was time to save their sorry lives.

I moved in on the one with the bayonet, got him in a good wristlock, almost broke the wrist before he released the blade, then kneed him in the groin. As he fell away I swung on the other, caught him right in the kisser. Turned back to the first and drop-kicked him in the chest, then back to the other with a kick to the balls. They were down, groaning, curled into little loser fetal positions. I was completely pissed. I took the blade, turned it with the pointy end toward myself, and gave each of them a good rap on the skull with the heavy handle. They flinched as I hissed into their faces. I told them I'd personally gut both of them, and if they survived the night at all I would court-martial their bullshit cowardly dangerous asses in the A.M. Then I kicked them both into their deep fighting hole, leaned over the edge, and told them if I heard or saw them during the night I'd drop a fucking grenade in there with them and if they didn't believe me to try it right now.

I must have sounded pretty real, because I didn't see either one until the dawn. Next morning they were the Contrite Twins. Apologized and said they'd do better. The SF lieutenant ambled by as they brewed coffee; he looked at them and growled. Off we went into the green, and they did indeed look and act like soldiers as we completed our mission of messing up Uncle Ho's trail.

I accompanied them back to their HQ the next day after we were lifted out of the triangle area, our part of Tollroad done for now. The more courageous of my two losers glumly told me I was right to kick their asses, apologized for both of them, and told me they had already had Article 15's and other troubles in their unit and if I told their Top what had happened they'd probably have some *serious* stuff thrown at them. I said nothing, but I was not unhappy with the way they had performed during the last day, night, and morning of the operation.

They were clearly nervous and subdued when we got to their unit, and I swear the Top sergeant's evil, knowing grin pissed me off as much as they had. He came sauntering down the gravel path toward us, waiting to hear how his two shit-birds had done with me.

"I've got something to say about these two soldiers you assigned to work with me, Sarge," I said briskly.

"I'll *bet* you do, LT," he replied as he looked over my two charges. They stood beside me, heads down.

"It might be better if they didn't work as a *team*, Sarge," I went on, "but all in all, they did a fine job for me. They were no problem, handled themselves well in the boonies, and I'd take either one or both of them with me again with no hesitation." I paused, enjoyed his discomfort and bewildered expression, and added for effect, "Tell your CO I said thanks."

He mumbled a "Yessir," managed a shaky about-face, and hurried away.

I shook hands with the two privates, caught their wary and hesitant grins, and left them.

Another Night Visitor

I took a photograph of a dead NVA soldier. I don't know why, exactly; something about the way he looked in death drew me to him. I was within a couple of months of ending my tour, and had seen plenty of bodies, but there I was with my camera, like some Fucking New Guy. The photo was not for *sale*, either. So my Instamatic captured him on the negative, and my mind's eye captured him, too. I still have both. The ruff-puffs (regional popular forces) took me to him the morning after another large ambush firefight on the east side of Highway 14, north of Pleiku. I had participated in the battle, but I did not kill him. He had no weapon, his ruck had been rifled, and he was alone in death. There were no more around him, and if there had been others wounded or in retreat they did not stop for him when they didi'd. He looked a little older than me, almost my size, lean and squared away. His uniform fit and was in good repair, and his feet were shod in workmanlike sandals. He had the obligatory before-battle haircut. His body was whole, indicating he had been hit with small-arms fire or light shrapnel. His shirtfront was covered with syrupy purple blood, and a smudge of it sat beneath his nose, on his upper lip.

He had made the long and dangerous trip down from the North to die there in the plowed dirt and shattered scrub trees, an infantryman for the PAVN, and somebody's son. As I looked at him I wondered about that, about whether he really did have a mom, whether she missed him and worried about him. Did they get telegrams? Did two uniformed officers knock on the door with official regrets? Was anyone, anywhere, aware that he had dutifully marched off into the green, never to return? While on the march did he receive letters from home—a Dear John, Mom's banal news about the college career of the boy next door, Dad's admonition to "make me proud"? I confess it was difficult to imagine him as part of his "World," with his family, to attribute to him dreams and aspirations. He was a dead NVA soldier, and I could accept him best as simply that. He was an interesting creature, to be sure, as so often we did battle with ambushes and booby traps, seeing only their tracer fire and explosions, only occasionally seeing *them*. You could see he pulled his pants on exactly the same way I did. He took care in tucking in his shirt, then buttoning his fly. He had come charging out of the tree line carrying some weapon, intent on killing us, maybe yelling in an adrenaline rush. When his chest exploded and he pitched forward, whom did he call out for as his face plowed the dirt and his last breath bubbled out with the blood?

It was as I first wrote this that I came to understand why I wanted to explore his death and speculate about it a little more than all the others I saw in Vietnam. It was his position. He lay on his left side, with his left shoulder, his left ear, and the left side of his head in the dirt. His hips were straight, his legs slightly splayed and bent at the knees. His right arm was bent at the elbow, the right hand in a loose fist near his face. The left arm was bent under the right, at his midsection, another fist. He did not look uncomfortable. During the years since I stood over him, no matter where or when I have seen someone dozing, child or adult, male or female, if they were in the same position my mind has immediately flashed to his image.

He created a negative in my heart, and my mind can print it any time.

Dipped

FIRST, you sweat. You sweat a lot: your hair, your arms, your hands, your back, the always-delightful trickle down your pant legs and into the tops of your boots. You sweat from the heat, even in the night, even in the rain, and you sweat from the tension and fear. You drape a green towel around your neck or a camouflage bandanna around your head, and you tie another bandanna somewhere on your weapon. It takes less than a few days to discover how right the other guys are when they tell you to lose the underwear. Just leave 'em hangin' and clangin', they air out better that way. The salt leaving your body during the day's hump leaves geologic patterns on your fatigue blouse for future study. You sweat, and your entire body is covered with a wet film.

Now take that wet body and go hump the boonies for a few days—hell, make it a week. Each sector of Vietnam has its own kind of terrain, but the many various types of dirt and mud can be found all over. Move your sweating body through the mud trails, through the mud streams, through the dripping drooping jungly branches that shine in anticipation and double as a launching point for various creepy-crawlies, including the ever popular leech. Walk point through the bamboo; the dry dust is an itching powder, the wet cuts on your hands an infection. Slip, fall, and roll down a rock-studded incline, clutching your weapon to your chest and cursing through a clenched jaw as you go. Take a break by leaning back against a rotting log, a reaching tree, a mound of dirt that might be an anthill. Try to get some Z's that night while crouching in a foxhole scooped out of sticky red clay, dirt clods falling from the collapsing sides. Wake in the morning with severe jungle bed-head, your face waffled and creased, your eyes red and dry, your teeth feeling like the heel of your boots. Scratch your itching balls with your fingers, the ones with fingernails that are black no matter how you try to clean 'em with the business end of your K-bar.

Get knee-deep in the middle of a rice paddy, the goal a distant tree line shimmering in the heat. Get ambushed. Rice is a big deal to the Viets, and what better way to fertilize it than with shit? So wade through their important rice, watch the green tracers arc out from the tree line at you, hear the screams and calls for help, feel the punching concussion from the falling mortars, and try to decide if you can mush-slog it another ten meters to the low dike for cover. If you can't, then you can eat shit . . . literally. As you try to keep your weapon dry and you watch the clumps of shit bob and wobble off your chest and arms while you do the rice-paddy low-crawl, you find yourself wondering, Why in the living *hell* are we always crossing a rice paddy in the open while the dinks sit in the shade of the tree line waiting for us to get close enough to shoot? Anger and frustration are good motivators, though, and these often help you not only get safely to the dubious protection of the dike, but also carry the fight to the dinks in the tree line. When a pissed-off grunt decides to verbalize his emotions over his lot in life and begins his tirade with "Well, I'll be dipped in shit," he's describing something that has already occurred.

Three, four days into the boonies, a couple of ambushes behind you, a couple of rice paddies under your chin, a couple of night mortar attacks in your portfolio; mix in many hours of hot rain, roll around in it all with survival-motivated gusto, and you find yourself sitting with your back against an abandoned VC bunker during a break in the hump. Look at your fingers, your crotch, your forearms. Scratch your wet scalp; spit a couple of times to check the color of the dirt. Lean your head back and feel the rotting wood trickle down your neck . . . and think of being clean.

Clean. You remember the smell of the crisp pillowcase on your bed the day your mom did the laundry. You run an imaginary hand down the front of your pressed button-down shirt, along the seams of your cords. You think of sitting in the early sunlight cleaning your nails with a pocketknife, your minty teeth tasting a stalk of fresh grass. Picture the way she walked toward you, her shampooed hair soft and flowing, smelling like summer all the way, her dress a pale yellow that shows all of her when backlit by a smiling sun. Look at her lips, her perfect eyebrows, the tiny curl of impossibly clean and fragrant skin behind her ear. Give yourself a snapshot of that time you sat in the shower with her, soaping each other all over and laughing as you played. Clean. You were clean.

A voice yells, "Saddle up!" You fill your lungs with the foreign, rotting, wet-firewood, dank, misty, heavy, wet, fertilized, corrupt, and filthy air of Vietnam, and you struggle to your feet. You know in your heart you will never be clean again.

Call for Fire

"**G**ET some!"

We'd say it when we fought. It was like the coach steaming by, hitting you on the ass, and grunting, "Tear their goddamned heads off, guys." We'd watch our artillery rounds crashing into a tree line where the NVA machine guns were and yell, "*Get some.*" We'd see our machine-gunner pumping 'em out, pumping 'em out into the wire during an attack and we'd yell "*Get some.*" We'd hunker down behind a dike and follow the arc of our bloop gunner's rounds as they lofted off, curved, then made their rapid descent and crunched into the enemy bunkers . . . and we'd yell, "*Yeah, get some.*"

One hot, clear, breezy afternoon I stood on a slight rise on the east side of Highway 14 south of Kontum during the tail end of a large ambush the NVA had sprung on a northbound truck convoy. I had called in artillery during the battle, walking it through the trees where the NVA support fires came from. Many of them died in the trees and in the cleared areas approaching the roadway. I don't remember any of our

trucks even stopping. As the fighting wound down, a severely
wounded NVA soldier was carried to the command area. He
had been shot in the head and was dying. An ARVN colonel
knelt beside him, spoke gently, and showed him a map. The
NVA licked his lips, pointed with a shaky finger at the map,
and laid his head on the stretcher. They gave him some water
and he died. The ARVN colonel explained that he had told
the NVA his war was over, there was nothing we could do for
him, and asked him to show us on the map where he had been
told to meet his unit as they regrouped after the ambush. The
NVA had pointed to a place in the hills where two ridgelines
and a stream converged. I checked my grid map against the
colonel's, found the spot, and called for several batteries to
fire a time-on-target (massed ARTY) on the place. It was
done, and as the volcanic roar of the massed artillery deci-
mated the area I was rewarded with the cry "*Get* some, LT!"

Then my Recon grabbed my shoulder, turned me around,
and pointed to the south and east. There the thick tree line
was split by a wide curve of rice paddies flowing off into the
distant hills. He handed me my binos, and as the far curve of
the paddy came into focus I saw almost a dozen khaki-clad
figures scrambling out of the trees to my left, crouching and
low-crawling across a low dike, heading for the safety of the
far tree line. NVA soldiers in the didi mode, bigger than shit.

I had my radio, the better to kill them with. Had a flight of
the new Cobra helicopter gunships standing by. Barked out
their call sign, received their laconic response, and told them
what we had discovered. It took only a few seconds for the
lead pilot to visually acquire the NVA soldiers involved in a
glorious lateral movement toward the rear, and a few seconds
more for me to give him the news that they were in a free-fire
area. Oh, my.

The scrambling NVA soldiers were almost three hundred

meters away, indistinct figures without my binos, but clearly visible for what they were. We stood on the rise beside the road as the Cobras came from our backs, screamed over our heads, and went in along the curving rice paddy. Their sides erupted into orange and black as their miniguns growled and their rockets roared, and as they pointed their deadly snouts toward the enemy soldiers the area around the dike exploded into flame, smoke, and geysers of mud and dirt. The NVA began that flailing, spastic, impossibly choreographed dance, flipping, tumbling; legs, arms, torsos, equipment all over the place. The Cobras blasted past them, made a steep climbing turn in formation, curved around, and went at it again. After their second pass there was no more movement. "I think we just ruined their entire day, two-niner," said the lead pilot over the radio as they swooped overhead and turned south.

"Get some," I answered.

The ARVN colonel did not want to send a unit out to check the bodies around the dike. He told me we had done a good job, the enemy had suffered a severe blow during and after the battle, and it was time to get back to base and have a cold one. We left them there, the dead NVA, their burst, torn, and torched bodies not even important enough to examine or count.

"Fuckin' A, LT," said some of the guys.

"Nice job, two-niner," said the American adviser to the ARVN's.

"Get some, Lieutenant," said my RTO.

I got some.

Chills

"RACKED with fever" is a good description. A Viet mosquito came softly buzzing out of the filth, sucked out some of my blood, and left me with malaria. The malaria took my body and mind, placed them on the rack, and cranked the rack up nice and tight. Never mind that I had been taking my Army-issue antimalaria pills faithfully, and yes that's one every bullshit day, and one the size of a blooper round once a week. Took 'em like a good soldier, became anemic, and caught malaria, both strains.

The first thing I noticed was how weak I'd become. Wondered if I was not getting enough exercise, or enough fish heads and rice; wondered if the war was just wearin' me down. Then came the fever, the chills, the sweats, the puking, the run-stumble to a handy spot while pulling forlornly at the fatigue pants. Finally my Recon and RTO dragged me into the 51st Medevac in Pleiku. The only doctor to be found was playing grab-ass with a round-eye nurse (who could blame him?) and mostly ignored us until Recon stood real close and had a word with him. Then the good doctor became very attentive and I was stripped, poked, stuck, and admitted.

My guys left me and I lay there with guys who had wounds. It is a horrible thing to be lying there with a body that is *not* bleeding, *not* cut, not gouged, punctured, burned, amputated, scalped, blinded, or in any other way visibly maimed or crippled, when you are in the midst of guys who *are*. I lay there breathing the same purple air, but felt ashamed. Stephen Crane knew exactly what he was talking about, and I lay there wishing I had something, some *blood*. I got a gloved finger stuck up my ass, got a thermometer jammed in my mouth, got the cramps and chills at the same time, and wondered how long I'd have to stay in that place of horror.

I felt selfish lying on a clean Army hospital sheet, eating hot hospital food, watching the goings-on in my ward. The nurses were a wonder to watch and hear, the black orderly a good man with his efforts to help me along by reading parts of his girlfriend's letter to me inch by inch. I let go of all humiliation and shame as I sat naked on the john in a large bathroom where the nurses bustled in and out getting supplies and giving me a cheery "Hey there." I trudged around like one of Tim Conway's characters, my stupid IV bottle squeaking along with me. Most of the wounded guys wouldn't ask. They'd look at me, see no bandage, see all my parts, and not ask. When someone *did* ask I would mumble, "Fucking malaria," in a voice designed to assure my listener I was completely aware of how entirely *lame* that was in a place where actual wounded guys were. They would nod and turn away.

The night sweats often brought visitors. One was a kid I had picked a fight with while home on leave before shipping out to Vietnam. Had words with him in the bleachers at a high school wrestling match, called him out. When I finally confronted him out in the parking lot I saw he was badly crippled—pale skin, hanging hair, skinny arms with small fists, bent and twisted legs propped up by angled metal braces. I wanted to let it go, but he wanted to fight, *wanted* it, he told me. His dad tried to stop it and the kid told him it was *his fight*. His dad backed off, and the kid swung and smacked me a couple of times while I tried to shrug it off and somehow get out of it, the crowd ugly, my humiliation complete. Finally one of his blows stung and I popped him. He straightened, I popped him again. He staggered, and I unloaded one right into his teeth. He reeled back, almost fell, but recovered and faced me again, his mouth bloody. This time when his dad said, "Enough," the kid put his fists down and nodded, a gleam of triumph and manhood in his eyes. He was escorted from the scene by a group of loudly proud supporters. I was left standing alone.

Sometimes in the sultry night my mom would be there. She cradled me and rocked back and forth, back and forth, her skin warm, her voice gentle. My dad knelt beside his fishing gear while he tied a Mirror-Lure to his line, his glasses up on his forehead. He said I looked skinny and much too serious, and wanted to know if I was up for some fishing; the mullet were running and there'd be lots of action. Both of my brothers stood at the end of my bed for a while one night, staring at me with curious expressions. Saw a girl's face and heard her laugh, but couldn't hang onto her or get close. Often when I awoke, the sheets around me soaked, my mouth cool and dry, I would remember that a very important question had come to me . . . but it was gone.

After a week I told the doctor I wanted to get back to my assignment, back to the ARVN unit and my Recon and RTO. It was close to Christmastime and there had been a lot of enemy movement reported. I didn't want to miss anything. He thought I was an idiot, but admired my determination. He told me the malaria was not through with me, then reluctantly let me go. I was issued new clothes, kept the old boots. I hitched a ride with some Signal guy out to Highway 14, found my guys. I felt alive, but weak, and had a sense that I had somehow done damage to my very core. I knew I would never be as strong as I had once been. The malaria would come for me again, hard the next time, and would rack me enough to make them send me to Japan. The night sweats were mine for a lifetime, but I didn't know it then.

All I knew was I was back with my guys, back at my job. There was a war, *he* was out there, and I wanted to breathe deep the purple wind while it blew.

Integrity

THE color is purple, and it cannot be defiled.

It is the combat award most respected, least desired. You can earn one by jumping off a truck and scraping your shins during a mortar attack, getting a small cut on your arm from a piece of flying metal, or losing a foot to a land mine. You can be awarded one for taking a bullet in the posterior, having your ear torn by a branch from an exploding tree, being burned on the neck by some of our napalm, or dying as your guts are blown out because you wrapped yourself around an enemy grenade to save your friends.

Some might argue that the integrity and value of it have been diminished by those who were awarded one in a contrived fashion—some rear-area type close to someone in the HQ tent, who got a cut over his eye after bumping into the latrine door and has this event falsely documented as having occurred during a rocket attack. I would respond by saying it certainly diminishes *them*.

Our guys who were POW's earned them, the guys you see

in front of the supermarket struggling in their wheelchairs earned them, and every single person you find named on the Wall earned one. The basic price for the chance to have one pinned on your chest is blood; the ultimate price needs no validation.

It is made up of pain, skin, muscle, nerve ends, bone, and blood folded into a mix of duty, courage, gallantry, decision, and honor. It is then left to harden in the glare of history, memory, and appraisal, and becomes an indestructible chunk of pride.

The color is purple, and it cannot be defiled.

Recon by Fire

SOLDIERS keep their memories of war because there is nothing else like it. They cling to memories of themselves as they were then, during it, doing, being part of war. Most carry it buried inside their hearts, theirs alone to examine or remember, theirs alone to feel the weight, the pain, the loss, the pride, the . . . value. Life in the World, after one has warred, struggles to equal the intensity.

The part of it I still wonder at was the sheer brutal destructive firepower available to me, an unimposing kid with a grid map and a radio. This is not the place for a discourse on the aesthetics of modern warfare or the creative energy used in the pyrotechnic destruction of things, so I'll leave it. However, part of the wonder comes from the self-saving feeling of being somehow right, of having done a warrior's work on the side of the good guys. As the years have gone by, of course, I have begun to temper the memories with the seasonings of cynicism, skepticism, maturity, and education. The memories survive, however, and with them many of the original pure feelings.

I was a Forward Observer. I knew artillery, its capabilities, the ranges. I knew how to call for fire, get a shot out there to look at, then adjust until it bracketed the target before I called for fire-for-effect. I learned how to bring it in at night, in the rain, in the middle of a battle's firestorm. I could adjust by sound, even in the triple-canopy cathedral. I could request it in a calm unhurried voice, in a hoarse whisper, or in an unbridled scream, and within seconds an avalanche of steel and fire would fall at my bidding.

I could also call in the helicopter gunships. They would swoop-clatter overhead and unleash their array of weaponry into any target area I specified. During bigger battles I had them make their runs on one axis while artillery fires fell from another.

Last came the fast-movers, the jet fighter-bombers. Where I worked, they were mostly but not only Air Force types. I could get different birds, but my favorite was the supreme asskicker of all time, the F-4 Phantom. There would be a Forward Air Controller flying around above the highlands in his little bird dog, and he and I would discuss my needs, and he'd introduce me to the big dogs. I know it was war, but watching those planes work, calling for them when you really needed them and seeing the results, was exhilarating and awesome.

Maybe it was my imagination (I heard later they tried to imitate Chuck Yeager) but it seemed all of the pilots were from someplace in the Deep South. I pictured them with a little plug of chew stuck between cheek and gum as they rolled that honker over on its side way the hell up there in that Indochinese-kinda sky, looked down at the white phosphorus the FAC had fired into the NVA bunkers, and drawled,

"Uh, yeeah, two-niner, I see that willy-peter. Understand the target is that tree line runnin' north–south on the edge of it. Ah, two-niner . . . I'd go ahead and uh, tay-yell your peoples to go ahead and . . . uh . . . keep they-are heads down now, 'cause we're comin' on down and it is . . . uh . . . gonna be *sweet*, ya know?"

Even knowing it was on the way, I'd always give a start when out of nowhere this charging, roaring, slamming loco-motive came streaking overhead, his bombs or other ordnance already falling free of the aircraft, banking sharply to give us a peek at his planeform, then climbing out on a thunder-rod, all-powerful and captivating. There would come an unreal pause, a suspension in the sound of the firefight. There would be a catch of breath, and the bombs from the long-gone Phantom would arrive.

Now. Now, you sorry little sonsabitches. Now you sit in your carefully constructed and camouflaged bunker behind your Chinese machine gun pumping bullets into the two or three of us you wounded with your first burst. Now you train it back and forth, looking for our medic, looking for the radio antennas that tell you where *I* am, you prick. You feelin' pretty good down there in that cool bunker, the red dirt packed nice and firm for your feet? Didn't you hear the loco-motive that just went past? Yeah, Nguyen . . . it was the 5:05 leaving Pleiku for Hanoi, Peking, and the big green parade in the sky. Look up and die, sucker.

It was not uncommon to call in the bombs close enough to force you to bury your face in the dirt, have your breath taken away, and hear spent shrapnel *whirrrr* by after the explosions. When the bombs went where you wanted them they usually had a dramatic effect on the situation, either ending the im-mediate battle, or at least forcing the enemy's heads down long enough for you to get up and into their faces or get your wounded and pull back. I could bring down a world of hurt, and I did.

Napalm. Do we all have stories of having to call it in so close little globs of the unlighted gray plastic stuff landed on our fatigues? Have we all heard the terms "crispy critters"? "Mushrooming fireball"? "Roiling, oxygen-sucking firestorm"? Did we sweep the area later and find their withered and charred asses twisted here and there like blackened scarecrows? Yeah, we did.

Memories of the power, of the brute force of war remain. Did responsibility, judgment, training, and control come with the power? Of course. That's why memories of war cling to us. It is a rare and precious thing, a horrendous and fascinating reality, which once experienced cannot be dismissed or forgotten. It is a wicked and heady drink, war, best tasted while young, and in a faraway land.

War is best in memory.

Be Gone

You're a liar, strange Bob.

You lied then; you lie now.

Lots of good boys died, strange Bob. Because of you.

You think now, now you vomit up your guilt in your book, you think that makes it okay, strange Bob? You got puke in your shoes, man.

Now you go and have a *summit*, Bob? You go and sit around and talk about how come you couldn't *stop* it, man? Did you worry about the shape of the table?

Lots of good boys died, strange Bob, because of you.

You one of the best and brightest . . . we just the *grunts*, man.

You had the power, best and spineless one . . . we had the *nerve*.

Lots of good boys died, strange Bob.
                                    Because of you.

You got puke in your shoes,
                And blood on your hands.

Transition

A GROUP of professional football players came to visit the sick and wounded Vietnam-kinda vets at the Camp Zama Hospital, in Japan. I heard they were coming, saw how excited everyone was, and wondered about my own feelings. I was embarrassed. I didn't want the visitors to stand beside my bed and make small talk about *what happened* or the World. Besides, they were larger-than-life pro ballplayers, our real heroes, the guys we watched on *This Week in the NFL* once a week when the hospital showed movies. The malaria took me down again, and I had been flown out of the Nam after eleven months in-country. Last week I had been in the green; now I was in a world of pain tinted with antiseptic cleanliness, caring nurses, stern doctors, and every imaginable wound. There was no in-between. I was *there*; now I was *here*, and heroic representatives from the World were coming to visit. It was too strange, and frightening.

I waited until I heard they were in the hospital, gave it a few minutes, watched the nurses bustling around, watched the IV bottles drip, watched the guy with no face struggle to a sitting position in anticipation, and swung my legs over the side of the bed. Somehow I had secured for myself a beautiful little acoustic guitar, and I picked it up and walked out of the ward. I wanted to be mobile, out and about in the hallways where I wouldn't be trapped.

There were three of them, escorted by a doctor, and walking shoulder to shoulder they filled the hallway. I was taken with how absolutely huge they were, huge, healthy, strong, and clean. They approached with steady purposeful strides, and looked at me with kindness in their eyes and smiles. I felt very small and grubby in front of them, and I guess I tried to smile back. I took a sliver of space along the wall and let them pass. The doctor made a friendly comment about the guitar and me making music and I felt really stupid as I walked away grinning, swinging it back and forth in front of me like an M-16 on full rock 'n' roll.

Later, when the hospital was quiet again, I replayed the encounter in my mind. It was then I remembered that the one in the middle had spoken. "Hi," he had said, and smiled. Back in the quiet safety of my bed, in the horrific normality of the ward with things once again in their predictable, comfortable routine, I realized it was Joe Namath. He had flown all the way around the world with those other guys to come and visit us, and it was pretty cool. They did good.

Joe Namath did good.

Met two wounded helicopter pilots, Carl and Ben. We hung around together in the hospital, and went on weekend trips when the doctors began allowing us to get out. We would go out to the little station, get on the first train that came along, and ride. Sometimes we would ride until the train stopped, with no way of knowing where we were or what we would do once there. No matter. The people of Japan were patient and gracious with us, and the memories are mostly good ones. We did the obligatory trip to downtown Tokyo, but did not do the bars, B-girls, or hooker scene. We went to the big hotels, found a real honest-to-God *malt shop*, and ate hamburgers.

I met a Japanese girl at the malt shop, a waitress. She was plainly pretty, very clean and groomed, and knew some English. She was almost as tall as I, and wore her long black hair parted in the middle. We kidded her bravely, the three of us, and she responded with such confidence it almost caused us to flee. She lured us with more milkshakes, and Ben actually asked her out. She said yes, and we did a lot of arm punching and sage nodding.

For some reason, Ben could not make it on the arranged date night, so I gallantly took his place. She met me with her brother in attendance (it *was* her first date with me), and we went to the Ginza district to shop and have dinner (table for three at a French restaurant where the menu was in Japanese; ordered Italian). Afterward her brother shook my hand and left us, and we walked to a lounge with three dance floors and a Japanese band that looked and sounded like the Beatles. We had drinks and watched the go-go dancers, and after a few minutes a guy in a tuxedo approached our table and asked me to dance. I sent him scurrying away with a curt reply, indignant, until the girl explained that young Japanese men felt it a privilege to dance with Americans so they could learn the latest dances. I sipped my drink and told her she had pretty ears.

When we slow-danced she came right up against me, fitting me in all the close ways, snug and soft and comfortable. We swayed together like that and my lips were soft against her neck and one of those pretty ears, and I could feel her thighs against mine and her breasts against mine and she was warm and smelled like girl and she made a sound like "Hmm-mmmm."

Her name was Chizu. She treated me with kindness and dignity, asked me for nothing, accepted from me what I was able to share, and held me tightly and close for a long moment the last time we were together.

One weekend Carl, Ben, and I spent a night in Tokyo in one of the biggest Western-style hotels. We spiffed up and went down to the busy well-appointed lounge. There we met a group of American girls, daughters of diplomats, business-men, and government workers who lived and schooled there. They were college-age girls, pretty, smart, and fashionably dressed. Someone introduced the three of us into the group and we sat with them around a low table for a few minutes. They were smart and breezy, we were raggedy and awkward. It took them approximately thirty-two seconds to learn we were Vietnam-kinda vets in hospital. Then they became cold, aloof, rude, and abrupt. Their brittle laughter was fueled by our presence, but it excluded and belittled us. They blew us off and we somehow separated from them, fixed grins on our stunned and burning faces.

What to do? Back up to the room for a cold one. Actually, the cold ones were real live chocolate (vanilla ice cream) sun-daes. They were on the room-service menu. We ordered, clobbered the first ones, then ordered the same thing again, to the polite consternation of the waiter. Very fine.

Lake Fuji Hotel, on the lake at the foot of the mountain. Got off at the end of a train ride, snow on the ground, early evening. Lost. Found the house of the cabdriver. He came out in his socks, explained he was having dinner, asked us to wait. Came out again and drove us to the hotel. He seemed very pleased, along with the desk staff, when we elected to stay there Japanese-style as opposed to "Western."

Beautiful wooden room with one glass wall looking out over the ice-crusted lake. Futons and tatamis. We stood incredulous at the simple purity of everything when the paper door was opened. The woman knelt on the other side of the door, bowed to us, stood with a tray of tea and cookies, stepped in, bowed again, placed the tray gently on a low table, went to the door, bowed again, and left. Each of us was quietly overwhelmed. It was just too clean, too warm and nice, and the people were too kind. I felt as if I shouldn't move too quickly or something would break, and I would be sent back.

Later we were shown the correct way to tie our robes and had dinner in a large room filled with young Japanese skiers who worked hard not to stare impolitely. We learned the art of drinking sake. I sat that night after the other two were asleep on the warm floor, sat with my fingers and cheek pressed against the cold pane of glass that separated me, in the exquisite room on one side, from the black frozen lake on the other.

I wondered at how thin the membrane.

Anointed

spit *vb* spit•ting **1** : to eject (saliva) from the mouth **2** : to send forth forcefully, defiantly, or disgustedly

I was disoriented when I deplaned at Oakland, California. It had been a long trip from Japan, before that from Pleiku. The trip and my physical condition had dragged me down. I was emotionally drained, even though I should have been elated at finally making it back to the World sort of in one piece. I had survived my tour in Vietnam, had done my duty, and now had come home. Like most young men in that strange military machine I had gone to war alone and returned alone, never really a part of one unit, close to only one or two other soldiers. I was a teenager when I joined, searching for answers and meaning. I came to know war, and *the* war, quickly, and was comfortable in that environment. Now I was coming home after three years, and it scared the hell out of me.

I had my duffel bag and a small camera bag, and was trying to make my way through the crowded airport lobby full of jostling people. Colors, sounds, smells, the size and shape of things all filled my senses as I tried to determine how to get to an area called GROUND TRANSPORTATION. The floor of the lobby was polished and I could place my feet haphazardly anywhere I wanted; there were no trip wires or mines. I could saunter right through the middle of the place, wide open, didn't have to seek shadow, defilade, hedgerow, or hardwood. People loosely scattered around a litter of bags on the floor turned out to be a group of college kids waiting for a flight, not a bunched-up squad caught by a mortar. I felt almost reckless in my freedom; it was intoxicating, and like someone slightly tipsy I tried to force myself to settle down and fly right, lest it all turn out to be too much of a good thing.

The ambush was carefully planned, staged, and executed. They knew the route I had to take, they knew they would blend in with the busy surroundings, they knew I would be easily identified, and they knew I would have my defenses down. The girl actually smiled as she approached. She was my age, I guess, with pale skin, lots of curly brown hair that fell beyond her shoulders, and a nice, open face. She had a thin mouth, which became a slit as she compressed her lips. Her eyes were bright and focused on me. She wore a heavy sweater, and denim pants sheathed her thick legs. I think she wore construction boots. Her partner was slightly older than me, tall and thin with greasy black hair parted in the middle of his skull and twisting outward behind his ears. He had a chin-beard, a purple mouth, bar-fight eyes, and a hickey on his neck. He wore an old Army field jacket covered with all kinds of different patches, not all military. He walked a step behind the girl. I saw them coming and made to step to their side, out of the way.

Suddenly the girl leaned toward me to eject saliva from

her mouth—to send it forth forcefully, defiantly, and disgust-edly. She sent it forth in that manner directly into my face. There was quite a lot, and as it globbed onto me I realized she had built it up in her mouth for some time behind that smile. Her spit was warm. After she ejected it forcefully, her mouth was free to begin forming words, which she screamed at me. I remember her angry red open face with all that hair blow-ing behind it, the oval of her mouth dark red and pink as it stretched and cupped and hollowed. Most of her words buf-feted and passed by me as noise, but I managed to capture a few, like "bastard," "killer," and "disgrace."

The girl's spit had barely finished its trajectory when the guy reached around her and pushed the contents of his large Coca-Cola onto the front of me from my chin to my crotch. There was enough of it to feel heavy as it hit me, and the smell was immediate and overpowering. Somehow my eye caught the image of a very American, sugary syrup flowing against the rows of combat ribbons on my chest, and there occurred one of those aural anomalies. As the soda washed against my chest and splashed outward, all other sounds in the room left me—even the girl's napalm-spewing mouth—and I could hear the drops of Coke pattering onto the floor and the polished toes of my black shoes.

I reacted like any target caught in the kill zone of a perfect ambush. I died. I was jolted to a rigid posture of horror and disbelief, my head back in a vain attempt to take my face out of the action, my arms askew and held out to the sides of my soaked torso, my feet stuck to the polished floor by the sheer brutality of the act.

My attackers had not planned their escape-and-evasion as well, however. They were not used to dealing with the adren-aline and emotional surges that come with close and intense confrontation. The girl, caught up in her cause, fueled by her own righteousness and audacity, wanted more from me. She wanted to grab my arm, pull me around, get her face close to mine, and smash those words she considered important into my brain, my heart. Her partner perhaps saw something in my eyes, as I had certainly seen the cowardice in his. He grabbed the girl by her shoulders and almost knocked her off her feet as he twisted and shoved her. As he did he turned his chin-beard back to me and shouted, "*Fuck you!*" Then they were gone, pushing and bumping their way into the crowded lobby and out of my sight.

One of the ways I had occupied my time in the hospital at Camp Zama the couple of weeks before I was sent home was to prepare my uniform. I wanted to go home in my class A's, the dress greens. It meant wearing a starched shirt with a tie, polished shoes, creased pants, and the dress jacket with officer's stripes and those cheap but priceless ribbons, but that's how I wanted to look when I got off the plane back in the World. I had attained the rank of First Lieutenant, but never intended to make a career of the Army. I had done my three years, done my war, and now I would be a civilian again. But coming back to the World from Vietnam I would be dressed in my class A's. If I'd been asked why, my explanation would have been fragmented and awkward. It had to do with respect. In Japan I had carefully acquired each part of the uniform, had taken it to an old tailor, had it cleaned and pressed and made right. Carefully pinned on the rows of ribbons in their correct order, made sure the patches on each shoulder were right, shined the brass. It fit my trimmed-down frame nicely.

I stood in front of the mirror in the airport men's room working with wet paper towels for a few minutes before admitting to myself there was no salvaging it. The spit and soda washed right off my skin, no problem, but not off the uniform. I rummaged around in a trash can, found a miniature plastic body bag, and rolled the loose and unresisting corpse into it. I couldn't bring myself to throw it away, though, so I stuffed it into my duffel and carried it home.

It had to do with respect.

AM

I'M convinced America changed completely and forever during the three years I was away in the Army. Oh, I know *I* changed, as a young man who had matured in the service and experienced the hard realities of war, but *we* changed, too. I don't think the actual window of change spans more than a year, two at most, but once the change began there was a spastic headlong rush to where we are now.

I came out of high school listening to the Beach Boys, the Beatles, the Supremes, the Everly Brothers, Aretha, the Stones, Ray Charles—you know. A local DJ named Rick Shaw played them for us on WQAM, ending the night around eleven with "Goodnight My Love." We would cruise the beach, totally wild with our shared six-pack of Miller beer. I was a radical in school, who surfed, played guitar, wore no socks *or* belt when I could get away with it, and got into the occasional fistfight. I went to the prom and spent all night trying to get a kiss from a nice girl. Then I joined the Army for the war. Lived in the military machine, got my tour in the Nam, went into the green.

When I returned to the World, my brothers and all their buddies who had remained home during those years decided to throw me and my friend Dave a coming-home party. They were proud of us, happy about our safe return, and they wanted to do something nice. One set of parents went conveniently out of town, so the party was at their house. When Dave and I arrived, things were cooking. The music was hard, driving, and slightly grating. The people were a little hairier than we remembered, but basically the same old gang. They didn't do much beer, though, preferring other substances they had been experimenting with. It became a kind of "fear and loathing" thing, and Dave and I were already uncomfortable when the host took us into a small room converted from a carport, where some bunks had been built into the wall. Our host had a couple of girls for us, he winked, because he knew we probably *needed* some of that. He indicated that these two girls, one already naked, the other shucking her clothes even as we watched, had taken a little something to make them feel very good, and were ready to do their patriotic duty. They were there for the taking, breasts, bellies, pubic mounds, nipples, tongues, fingers, smiles. They beckoned to us, moving to the hard music, their eyes shining. We made a hasty but dignified and appreciative complex tactical maneuver known in the military as hauling ass . . . or in the Nam as "didi-mau most ricky-tick."

We borrowed somebody's car, bought a six-pack of Miller, put ol' Rick Shaw on the radio, and drove to the beach to try to pick up girls.

Tin

I CAN'T help but think of that ol' Cowardly Lion when I think of my medals. The best and brightest wizards reached way down into their bag to pin them on me, but they were humbugs, weren't they? I have a photograph of General Peers pinning one to my boyishly proud chest, but in typical Army fashion the paperwork was never submitted, so the medal does not exist. Some of the others I received came from a government that no longer exists; its leaders live in defensive and indignant luxury in the free world. They are symbolic, it is argued, something hard and tangible to represent and recognize those hard and intangible moments that occur in a reality that can never be duplicated. In truth, they hold a real but undefined meaning for me, an equation of price and value that has no finite balance or sum.

I didn't throw my medals over the White House fence.

I gave them to my mother. She put them away someplace, nice and quiet.

The Wall

I WORE my dogtags for years after I left the green. I could pull them out still—in their rubber sleeves to keep them from making any death rattle—and read the information stamped there with certainty. They clearly stated who I was, what I was . . . my name, serial number, blood type, and religious preference. I don't wear them now, but they hang where I can see them, along with a rusty P-38 waiting to liberate some C-rats.

Through the years I have read everything I could get my hands on about the Vietnam War, trying to find . . . something. As with many things in this dangerously free country of ours, every writer brings to his or her work their own point of view or opinion, so the reference library I have collected is all over the place. None of it diminishes the war for me, or takes away the intensity. None of it convinces me we were wrong, either—we, the guys on the ground, the guys in the green with rifles. Misdirected perhaps, misled, misinformed, ignorant, naive, culturally blind . . . sure. Criminal, cowardly, corrupt, drug-ridden, racist? Not as much as has been portrayed. Most of what I saw was just regular young guys trying to do the best they could under ill-defined and difficult circumstances, trying not to shame themselves, and trying to get home where they belonged.

I went to the Wall after a long struggle, and found Butchy's name. Found a couple of others, too. Found myself swept and buffeted by an avalanche of willy-peter emotions—all the old feelings. I moved carefully, watching, searching, listening, considering each step before I made it as if walking point. I tried to capture all the names as my eyes swept the reflective face of the Wall, tried to imagine their lives and deaths, tried to gauge the cost in terms of raw emotion. I felt the loss, and reconned back to Walter Guy "Butchy" Burkhart as my eyes found his name shining there.

I was the one who suggested he become a Lurp. He was on his way to the Nam, he was an airborne infantry grunt, and I wanted to give him sage advice to help him survive his tour.

"Don't get lumped in with some line outfit," I said with the confidence of one who has *been there*. "Volunteer for the Lurp teams, you know, the Long-Range Recon Patrols. Sure, they go out into enemy territory in small groups and spend a couple of days in truly hairy situations, but they're trained and equipped for it and they've got unbelievable support lined up, and they pick and choose when and if they want to get into a fight. Believe me," I continued—and why wouldn't he?—"the Lurp teams have the lowest percentage of guys gettin' wounded or killed. Even though they do special balls-to-the-wall stuff, you'll be able to have a good tour and come home in one piece."

He nodded in acceptance of my assurances. When he hugged me good-bye he held it a moment longer and a little

tighter than I'd expected, like he was trying to tell me something. Then he was gone.

He wasn't even gone a month, and I couldn't believe how
excited I was, waiting to see him again. We had been friends
all our lives, close like brothers, the years and experiences of
growing up a bond strong, good, and real. Those of us who
knew him knew he should never have been in the military. If
out of our whole group we voted for the one person who for
sure should have never been a soldier going off to war, it
would have been him. He was a gentle and funny boy, smart
and open, always seeking answers to questions most of us
never asked. His was not a graceful adolescence. He was shy
and awkward around girls, and often socially clumsy. On
weekend mornings he wore a bathrobe over pajamas, which
those of us who slept in their BVD's found hilarious. He loved
June bugs and rocket ships, was always puttering around with
electric and mechanical projects in his garage, and participated in outdoor things like fishing and hunting with us
mostly because *we* did. We were pleasantly surprised when he
got a "serious" girlfriend in high school (the perfect match:
she was angular and pretty, a student of arcane poetry, a girl
who wore black berets, a girl who was against "the war"). He
was healthy and strong, with clear pale skin and curly brown
hair, wondering eyes, and a quick smile. His draft notice came
and he decided to join up rather than wait. He asked for nothing special, and eventually became an eleven-bravo . . . airborne.

In Vietnam he was assigned to the 75th Infantry (Ranger),
and volunteered for the Lurps. On his first mission, in the
province of Binh Thuy, his team was involved in a running
firefight, and he was wounded in the neck. They got him out
all right, but he was paralyzed from the neck down, critical.
The Army flew his parents to Saigon because of his condi-

tion, and they managed to see him. Then, with the second hand on his clock literally ticking away, the number of words left to him in conversation extremely finite, he made his mother listen to a message for *me*. He wanted her to be sure to tell me "he was pretty sure he got a couple of them before they got him." Then, while being moved from one hospital to another, he died.

I remember his father, a quiet, serious engineer type, coming across the street from his home to tell me when they first got the news his son had been wounded. All of my emotions surged through my body and came out of my mouth with the brilliant observation, "Well, at least now he'll come home." His father, openly crying, responded, "Yes . . . but *how*?"

I'll tell you how. He came home in a box. The box was draped with our flag, escorted by a living soldier sharp and respectful. Inside he lay with his eyes closed and his hands folded across his chest. He was dressed in his green, very formal, with a neat row of ribbons which included the Air, the Bronze, and the *Purple* one, which validated the wound that killed him. I don't know if they actually put his Corcoran jump boots on his feet. I *do* know I was impatient for the day of the funeral, impatient to *see* him. I missed him, and even though I understood I could not . . . visit . . . with him, I wanted to be with him, and *see him again*.

I had to wait a few minutes while others gathered around the casket. I felt uncomfortable, unwelcome, seeing in the glances from his parents and sisters that unanswerable question: Why *him*? Why not *you*? Finally he lay there alone for a moment. Heart pounding. I stood close to him. He looked just like himself, and I saw he had grown a light mustache while away. He was very quiet, and so was I.

They did the military honor guard and the folded flag thing at the gravesite. His mother got the crisply folded flag, our ears got the meaningless words from the sky pilot. We stood on an exquisitely manicured expanse of lawn under a hard blue forever sky as he was lowered into the green. The rigid-shouldered straight-backed bugler blew "Taps."

"Taps" is a haunting and lonely call for evening reflection over the darkening sky on some faraway military base.

"Taps" is a sad and promising requiem sounded for a dead president and the Unknown Soldier at Arlington.

But there is nothing like the sound of that sad, sorry, hard, ass-kicking, heart-wrenching son of a bitch blown on a clear living day with the kid you grew up with dressed as a soldier and lying cold and gone forever in a box at your feet.

We were both nineteen years old.

I didn't go to the parade, years later. Didn't watch it on TV, either. Don't want to see guys cryin' all over the place. Don't want to hear Bob or Jane or any of the best and brightest apologize. They are liars. I don't want to go on a "Peace Journey" back to Vietnam, and I don't have a "Viet Vet" bumper sticker.

But I respect those who do.

I *do* have an old Harley-Davidson painted in six shades of camouflage green, and I ride the purple wind with quiet pride.

ACKNOWLEDGMENTS

For help in making this book a reality, I would like to thank:

My agent, Jane Gelfman, for her straightforward encouragement, her tenacity, and her guidance.

My editor at Plume, Gary Brozek, for his faith in my work, his acumen, and his courage.

My wife, Helen Smallwood, for always believing in me. *Satis magnum alter alteri theatrum sumus.*